Walking Into A Hug

Walking Into A Hug

52 weeks to a home that's more embracing

By

Janene E. Ustach

CFI
Springville, Utah

This is not an official publication of The Church of Jesus Christ of Latter-day Saints. The opinions and views expressed herein belong solely to the author and do not necessarily represent the opinions or views of Cedar Fort, Inc. Permission for the use of sources, graphics, and photos is also solely the responsibility of the author.

ISBN 13: 978-1-59955-225-5
Published by CFI, an imprint of Cedar Fort, Inc., 2373 W. 700 S., Springville, UT 84663
Distributed by Cedar Fort, Inc., www.cedarfort.com

Library of Congress Cataloging-in-Publication Data

Ustach, Janene E.
   Walking into a hug / Janene E. Ustach.
      p. cm.
   ISBN 978-1-59955-225-5 (alk. paper)
   1. Family--Religious aspects--Church of Jesus Christ of Latter-day Saints.
   2. Family--Religious aspects--Mormon Church. 3. Family--Religious life.
   I. Title.
   BX8643.F3U88 2009
   248.4'89332--dc22
                                    2008041856

Cover design by Angela D. Olsen
Cover design © 2009 by Lyle Mortimer
Edited and typeset by Natalie A. Hepworth

Printed in the United States of America

10 9 8 7 6 5 4 3 2 1

Printed on acid-free paper

First and foremost this book is dedicated to all my friends and family who skipped parenting classes with me in the premortal life. I sure hope we were having a lot of fun, because we are definitely paying for it now! I hope this book will give us all ideas and insights into what we missed. There is no way to cover everything, but maybe this book will give us techniques and ideas to make parenting more fun and manageable from here on out.

Next to my husband, Steve, for having to deal with my parenting wrecks. I'm sure he never skipped pre-parenting classes, and I believe he would do a much better job parenting our children than I do. You are a wonderful husband, father, and friend (along with all the other hats you wear). I love you always. Thank you for so many "wonderful" years.

And finally, to my children: Nick, Matt, Trent, and Katelyn. This book is for you, so that my grandchildren will turn out perfect. Even though I wasn't the perfect parent, I did the best I could. I hope you will learn from my mistakes and be an even better parent to your children. I love each of you dearly, and hope that when you walk into our home you feel that you are "walking into a hug."

Acknowledgments

Thank you to my children for making my attempts at motherhood so complicated that I would seek out ideas and advise to be a better mother.

Thank you to my husband for your endurance, support, never-ending love, and time spent polishing the words in this book.

Thank you to three great women who reviewed the early draft of this book and gave me their honest feedback:

Cindy for all your wonderful suggestions, and for being there when I needed a shoulder to cry on. Thank you for being a friend, and for not hurting me when we play basketball.

Amy I admire you for your steadfastness and insight of the gospel. I treasure our friendship and appreciate the example you are to me.

Nikki for still being in the trenches of motherhood. I admire your ability to endure with a smile, and I marvel at your testimony and grasp of the gospel.

Thank you to all!

Contents

Introduction

At some point in our lives we catch glimpses of what our time spent in the premortal existence was like. These glimpses may be times of déjà vu; or perhaps a person we meet has a certain familiarity; or even an investigator of the gospel recognizes truths they had embraced in a premortal life.

I, too, have moments of recognizing my premortal existence; however, it's never quite so sentimental or life-changing as others experience. It's quite simply in my every day attempts at being a parent that I realize I must have "ditched" the parenting classes taught in the premortal life. I suspect that parenting classes followed choir and singing classes. While I intentionally skipped choir and singing classes (together with a lot of my friends and relatives), I, unfortunately, never made it back in time for the parenting class.

This came to light a few years ago when my four children instigated a mutiny. My two elementary-aged children stomped onto the school bus that morning upset because they had gotten up late, didn't get the breakfast of their choice, and the morning was rushed and chaotic. My teenager left next, in a huff, after giving me the silent treatment all morning for being sentenced to a week of grounding (of course it was my fault). My eleven-year-old exited promptly thereafter, slamming the door out of anger because I refused to make him another sandwich that he wouldn't eat anyhow. I guess I was justified when I finally broke down in tears, and remorsefully admitted that "yes," I had disregarded the parenting classes in the pre-earth life and had no parenting skills whatsoever.

This caused me much unrest as I always aspired to be the "best" mom. While I was growing up, I liked to watch a popular family television show.

During one episode, the kids in this family stated that coming home from school was like "walking into a hug." From that moment on, that was my motto, and I wanted my future children to feel like they were walking into a hug whenever they came home. I was naïve enough to think that my future children would want to stay right by my side, listen to every word of my advice, do everything I asked, and shout accolades to my name. Instead, they now just shout other things that aren't fit to print.

After the day of my epiphany, I realized that had I missed out on some pretty important information in the premortal existence and I had a lot of make-up work to do. I resolved to gain all the knowledge I was lacking before my kids grew up. I started reading everything I could get my hands on that had to do with parenting. I picked the brains of friends and relatives, and whined and cried on a lot of friends' shoulders. However, despite all the knowledge I think I have gained, I cannot seem to implement the best techniques, at the right time, and with the right child.

So I am writing this book for myself and all my friends who "ditched" parenting classes with me. I am by no means an authority on child rearing. In fact, I feel like a hypocrite writing this book and have almost abandoned this whole idea on several occasions. Those were usually the times I would be in tears admitting that I was not cut out to be a mother. But what kept me going was my desire to have a peaceful and enjoyable home where family members feel like they are walking into a hug.

About This Book

This book is a workbook. For each week there is a suggested goal to help you broaden your parenting skills. Below the goal are suggestions, ideas, and clues to make it successful, and how to implement it as a permanent method to your parenting. The next page has blank lines for you to record how the week went. After you try the suggested techniques for a week, make entries as to whether you detected any noticeable change in your home:

+ Did you notice your children behaving differently?
+ What were your children's responses to the technique?
+ What would you do differently next time?
+ Did you learn anything from this experience?

If you are really serious about learning to be a good parent, you need to review and reflect upon the results of your efforts. By writing down your experiences and thoughts, you may come across choice techniques that will really help you in being a better parent and raising a great family

This book is written from my perspective of being a mother. However, the principles herein apply equally to both mothers and fathers. In fact, if your spouse is willing to work through this book with you and also implement the techniques, you could expect to see significant improvements in your home and family life. Your efforts are doubled, thus your results should also be doubled.

For some of the goals, it will be helpful to share with your family the principles you will be applying throughout the week so they will recognize and assist in your efforts. This may best be accomplished by a family meeting (see chapter 3, "Family Night").

Throughout the book references are made to the "FHE Resource Book" which is an abbreviated title for the *Family Home Evening Resource Book*, published by The Church of Jesus Christ of Latter-day Saints. This is a wonderful resource manual, great for all families, and has suggestions for adapting lesson material for children of all ages. Not only does it discuss the topic for that week, it supplements with scriptures, stories, and lessons about Jesus.

If you don't already have this resource book, you can purchase a copy at your local LDS Distribution center, or order one online at www.ldscatalog.com (see Gospel Study Resources: Books and Manuals) for a nominal price.

Although there is a goal for every week of the year, I would assume that some of you may have already mastered certain parenting techniques and do not need every topic that is given; or that some of the challenges presented may not be a problem for you right now. If you do not need to work on a specific week's focus, simply go on to the next chapter or work on a previous technique that you want to develop further or possibly with a different spin.

There are some specific areas that parents have problems with, such as the telephone, fighting in the car, or sibling rivalry. Unfortunately, I do not have the cure-all for these situations because there is not one perfect answer. However, I do provide ideas for you to apply and hopefully you will find the right answer for your family. Again, if these areas are not a problem for you, move on.

Make sure you take the time to read and ponder the quotes and scriptures provided at the beginning of the week's goal. These quotes and scriptures are very powerful and contain great promises, advice, and blessings that can be yours by incorporating these parenting practices into your family.

Do not be disheartened if a technique you think will be successful falls flat on its face. With some methods you will notice a change, and with others you might not. In learning and practicing these new techniques, you may even be inspired with the ideal parenting technique for your specific family situation. Whatever your experience may be, record the results on the lines provided.

BE WARNED AND FOREWARNED

There will be resistance as you try these different parenting methods. Children rebel at change. There will still be days of disorder and confusion.

Your children will make this project hard—that is their job (and they do it so well!). When this occurs, grit your teeth, smile, and refuse to throw in the towel. Remember, you nor your children are perfect. You are still learning to be a parent, and your children need your help to learn and grow through childhood. Don't say you weren't warned!

ONE PARTING THOUGHT

In working on the goals in this book, you need to include Heavenly Father. You need His help in this project. You need to develop a relationship with your Heavenly Father, and counsel with Him every morning and every night, and sometimes in-between. Let Him know that you want to be a better parent, and that you want to have a loving family, a loving home life, and a home where His spirit is welcome. Ask for His help in these weekly goals. Share with Him the problems you are having with a particular child or issue, ask for His advice, tell Him you have done all that you know how, and turn the problem over to Him; and *then* listen and watch for His answer to come.

Heavenly Father does want you to succeed and to discover the best way possible for teaching the children he has entrusted to your care.

I once heard that all families have problems, but the difference between a good family and a *great* family is their ability to deal with problems and to learn from them. That said . . .

Go forward and learn to be a great parent and create a home where your children feel like they are "walking into a hug."

Simply Smile

*"Smiling is good for the soul. Smiling brings a glow
to our countenances that radiates to others."*

JAMES E. FAUST

GOAL: Smile

We hear repeatedly that a mother's attitude influences the entire family's attitude. Smiling is very simple. It does not require any advance planning, and its results are detected almost immediately. It makes the person smiling and everyone around him feel better. Go ahead and smile right now—a big heart-felt smile—and feel the burden lift off your shoulders. Keep that smile going all week long.

Smiling is consistently my recommended starting point in my books because it is a basic concept that is essential for our self-esteem; and it can be used as a support at anytime. While working on later goals, if you find yourself getting frustrated and wanting to give up because your attempts are not going as smoothly as you had hoped, use smiling as your fallback— simply smile!

Smile while you are:

+ driving the carpool
+ changing diapers
+ doing the dishes
+ folding the laundry
+ paying bills
+ scrubbing the toilets
+ mopping the floor
+ making dinner
+ wearing all the many hats a mother has to wear

When times get really tough, and they will, *simply smile*. Smile while telling yourself that you are happy, that you enjoy being a mother, that you are a good parent, that you can do this, that you love your children, and that your children are great.

Just *keep smiling*!

Simply Smile

....

....

....

....

....

....

....

....

....

....

....

....

....

....

....

....

....

....

....

....

....

....

....

....

Plentiful Praise

"Praise your children more than you correct them.
Praise them for even their smallest achievement."

EZRA TAFT BENSON

GOAL: Catch your children in the act of being good, and envelope them in well-deserved praise.

Children respond more to praise than any kind of constructive criticism or negativism. Praise, in its simplest form, raises your children's self-esteems and makes them feel accepted and competent.

This week, praise your children for *everything* good they are doing. Praise them for:

- getting up on time
- getting dressed by themselves
- making their bed
- cleaning up a mess
- playing nicely
- sharing
- pouring their own milk
- getting chores done quickly
- being quiet while you were on the phone
- having to be asked only once to do something
- doing their homework diligently

Make a practice of praising the *act* and not the child. Don't say, "I love you for cleaning your room," but rather, "Your room looks great. You did a good job cleaning up." You want to be careful not to infer that you only love your children when they are doing good. You love them all the time, but their good acts deserve to be praised. Don't be shy about "singing these praises" to others; it is even all-the-better if your children overhear you.

Learn to praise your children for *all* things. This principle of plentiful praise will be referenced within other topics throughout this book; and, when used in conjunction with these other topics, will make the lessons more meaningful to both you and your children.

Plentiful Praise

date..............................

....
....
....
....
....
....
....
....
....
....
....
....
....
....
....
....
....
....
....
....
....
....
....
....

Family Night

*"Now here are the blessings promised by a prophet
of God for those who will hold weekly [family] home
evenings: 'If the Saints obey this counsel, we promise
that great blessings will result. Love at home . . . will
increase. Faith will be developed in the hearts of the
youth of Israel, and they will gain power to combat the
evil influences and temptations which beset them.' "*

EZRA TAFT BENSON
as quoted by L. TOM PERRY

GOAL: Block out one evening a week and make family night a priority where the Spirit is invited to dwell.

The promises by President Benson of holding weekly family home evening are so tremendous that every parent should strive to have these blessings for their family. If you don't hold regular family night, this week is geared toward making the preparations for it to happen. If you do have regular family night, use this week to focus on inviting the Holy Ghost into your time together.

If you would like family night to happen regularly, you *must make assignments* that involve everyone in the family. (One friend told me that their family night never happened until they made an assignment chart and then it "automatically" happened every Monday night.) If you don't already have one, make an "assignment chart" that shows what each family member is responsible for on family night. This assignment chart could be a simple planning wheel that rotates each week (see *FHE Resource Book*, "Using a Planning Wheel for Assignments", p.164 for more suggestions), or a wooden plaque, or a laminated picture with velcro name-attachments where names get changed each week. Assignments could include:

+ conducting
+ prayers *(opening and/or closing)*
+ scripture
+ music
+ lesson
+ activity

+ simple family business (see chapter 31, "Family Council")
+ treat

We have also incorporated "recognition time" where we recognize each person in the family for some accomplishment, be it big or small. The person conducting chooses those who wish to recognize others either by raising their hand or by reading the written "recognitions" that have been collected in a jar during the week.

Encourage all members to attend family night. "It often takes a seemingly superhuman effort to get everyone together for family home evening. You may not always feel like praying when you finally do get together, but it will pay great dividends if you persevere."[1]

Make sure there are no interruptions during your family night. Let the phone go to the answering machine; do not turn on the television or other forms of entertainment, unless they are part of your family night.

A dear friend enlightened me when she shared that the most important thing for family night is to *give your children the opportunity to feel the spirit.* To do this, you must have well-planned lessons and activities that invite the Spirit into your home. Family night could also include:

+ anonymous acts of service
+ teaching values
+ discussing spiritual topics
+ acting out scripture stories
+ playing question games with gospel themes
+ sharing your testimony and uplifting stories
+ planning for upcoming events
+ having fun together as a family

Make family night a family tradition, make it fun, make it uplifting, and invite the Spirit.

Notes:
1. James E. Faust, "Enriching Our Lives Through Family Home Evening," *Ensign*, June 2003, 3.

Family Night

date...................................

....
....
....
....
....
....
....
....
....
....
....
....
....
....
....
....
....
....
....
....
....
....
....
....
....

Schedule for Structure

*"Some people use a rather structured approach and find
it provides the security and direction they enjoy."*

S. BRENT SCHARMAN

GOAL: Make a *written* schedule that you would like to follow for a
particularly difficult time of the day, and follow this schedule for the
entire week.

A schedule is a marvelous tool that benefits the parents, probably
more than the children. If you are having a particularly difficult day, you
can depend on the schedule to get you through a period of time what you
would otherwise dread.

Determine your most difficult time of the day with your children.
Your most difficult time could be:

- morning time
- just before lunch
- nap time
- chore time
- after school
- before dinner
- bedtime
- whatever time of the day you find most challenging

Sit down with pen and paper and write what needs to happen and at
what time *you* want it to happen. Review this schedule with your children.
Post the schedule in a place where everyone can see it and review it often.
If your children are young, consider making a chart with pictures that they
can understand.

You may be tempted to schedule several hectic times of the day, but
don't do that just yet. You and your children will likely get frustrated and
overwhelmed. For now, just choose one time of the day and really work on
that area for this week. As the week goes on, make adjustments to your
schedule as needed, still striving to provide structure that reduces the
chaos.

The most important thing to remember when you have a schedule in place is to be flexible. There will be days that schedules just cannot be followed, but make sure this is the exception and not the rule. When your schedule doesn't work as you planned, and mayhem sets in, "simply smile!"

Schedule for Structure

date ....

....
....
....
....
....
....
....
....
....
....
....
....
....
....
....
....
....
....
....
....
....
....
....
....

Family Rules

*"Family rules must be established and observed before
the blessing of family harmony can be attained."*

LAYNE E. AND JANA SQUIRES FLAKE

GOAL: Make a *written* set of family rules and expectations.

Just as a civilized society needs rules to peacefully exist, so does a family. Rules help children feel safe, secure, and protected. However, the rules must be *written* down in a book that every family member can refer to them often so ignorance cannot be asserted.

You will need to purchase a sturdy notebook that will be used and referred to throughout the years. You should label the book such as the "Barker Family Rule Book" so it looks official and does not get misplaced.

It is essential to begin this week with a family meeting to discuss rules. Begin the meeting with a lesson on why rules are important. Refer to the *Family Home Evening Resource Book* for ideas.[1]

Next, have your children recite to you what family rules now exist. Write these rules down in the notebook, *leaving at least two lines between each rule*. (These blank lines will be used for establishing consequences later, if needed.) Remember that the rules should be short, clear, and to the point. Make sure to state how, where, when, why, and by what time, if appropriate.

During the meeting, discuss other rules you should implement in your family. Make sure to discuss why these rules are important to your particular family. If you allow your children to participate in establishing the rules then they are more willing to obey them.

There are different kinds of rules: *Mandatory rules* are rules that, if broken, may have deadly consequences, such as crossing the street without an adult or using the stove without an adult present. Mandatory rules also include God's laws or commandments which are not optional, including laws of honesty and chastity, the Word of Wisdom, and Sabbath observance.

Discretionary rules are rules that you expect your children to obey, but offer the opportunity for children to learn to make their own decisions.

It is not necessary that your children differentiate between mandatory and discretionary rules. But as a parent this may act as a guideline for determining those rules that are absolute and others where the child will participate in their establishment and enforcement.

Not all rules require a consequence, especially up front. If you already have an established consequence for a broken rule, write it down in the empty lines after that rule.

Rules to consider:

- curfew time
- household chores
- guidelines for television and electronic games
- dinner time rules
- obeying the Word of Wisdom
- attendance at church meetings
- seminary attendance
- not dating until of the approved age
- weekly family home evening and attendance
- nightly family prayer and scripture study
- loving the Lord and one another
- no quarreling
- obeying your parents
- no swearing
- respecting each other's privacy and belongings
- treating people with respect
- establishing education expectations

One family with older children uses a Family Rule Book but takes it a step further. After a rule has been set, each family member signs their initials beside the rule acknowledging the rule and agreeing to abide by it. In addition to rules, this family adds "expectations" and "conflict resolutions" to their Family Rule Book. These may include criteria for how a particular chore is to be accomplished, such as cleaning the bathroom; or not allowing your daughters to share clothes because the clothes are often returned damaged, or not returned at all; or that when your son wants to make his famous, but messy, spaghetti dinner, he is expected to completely clean up afterward. When your children affix their initials beside a rule or expectation they tend to take the rule more serious, knowing they will be held fully and solely accountable.

Monitor your family life throughout the coming week. If a situation arises that would benefit from another rule or expectation, write it down and discuss it with the family at the next opportunity. Remember to have family members initial the rules and expectations if appropriate.

Again—all rules need to be written down.

The rule book needs to be reviewed by the family periodically, perhaps a couple times each year, to refresh everyone's memory and to edit or add new rules that have evolved since it was last reviewed.

Notes:

1. *Family Home Resource Book,* Lesson 2, "The Commandments—Gifts from a Loving Father," 7; or Lesson 20, "A House of Order," 89.

Family Rules

date ....

....

....

....

....

....

....

....

....

....

....

....

....

....

....

....

....

....

....

....

....

....

....

....

Consistent Consequences

*"Choices have consequences. In some measure these choices
will affect not only the rest of your life but all eternity."*

JAMES E. FAUST

GOAL: Decide the consequences for all broken rules, and *consistently* follow
the three steps for administering consequences.

How contrary this sounds, you *do not* want your children to always
be obedient. In fact, the key to successful child-rearing is to *rejoice* when
your children break the small, discretionary rules. Be glad they are making
mistakes, because this is how they *learn* and how we as parents *teach* right
from wrong. As children grow and mature, they will inevitably make
mistakes. If they are not held accountable, they will not learn to take rules
seriously. Thus, when they are held accountable for the small and simple
rules, they make better choices when it comes to the bigger, mandatory
rules. This process eventually teaches children to become responsible
adults. Look forward to the opportunity this week to *guide* your children.

Decide on consequences. Write, or review, the consequences for
broken rules in your Family Rule Book. Attempt to choose a consequence
for breaking each rule such as:

+ If your child jumps on the furniture, then have him take care of
the furniture he was abusing by dusting, polishing, or vacuuming
it.
+ If they are unkind to the family pet, then they must take care of
the pet and give it extra attention and love.
+ If they are mean to a sibling, then they must apologize and be
extra nice by doing one of the sibling's chores.
+ Potty words can be "washed" out of a dirty mouth.

Sometimes related consequences aren't possible, but you can be
creative—use a time out, bestow an extra chore, have the offender write
affirmations, or any other consequence you feel would best guide your
children.

There are three steps for administering consequences to a child.

1. **Give a warning.** When your child makes a wrong choice,

immediately give them a warning. A warning is important because it gives your child a chance to change their direction and make a right choice. A warning may be vocally counting to three, using your fingers in counting to three, or saying a word you have established as your "warning word." Never count to ten or use halves in your counting. This only gives your child time to analyze the situation and consider a power struggle rather than simply obeying. If your child obeys what you have said after the warning, *praise* him for choosing the right.

2. **Act promptly.** If after giving one warning, your child continues to test you, you must *act promptly, without blame and without emotion,* to administer the consequences. You cannot "wait until Dad gets home." You must follow through with the consequence on the spot. If you wait until later, the misdeed will be forgotten, and the consequence won't be related to the transgression. Avoid placing any kind of blame as it only creates ill feelings. Any emotion that you may show, such as anger, frustration, or sadness, makes the child believe that they have triumphed in getting you upset.

3. **Follow-up with increased love.** The scriptures tell us that after correcting a child we need to follow up with "an increase of love toward him whom thou hast reproved" (D&C 121:43). After receiving punishment, spend a little bit of time with your wayward child discussing their actions, how they should apologize if needed, what they learned, and how they can do better next time. Make sure you tell them that you love them.

Children need to experience the consequences and be accountable for their poor choices and misbehavior. If children can predict what their consequences will be, they can learn to make better choices in the future. Remember to *rejoice* when your children misbehave, as they are giving you a chance to *guide* them.

Consistent Consequences

date ....

....
....
....
....
....
....
....
....
....
....
....
....
....
....
....
....
....
....
....
....
....
....
....
....

Love at Home

*"Tell your children that you love them and that you
are so happy to have them in your family."*

PATRICIA P. PINEGAR

GOAL: Shower your children with "I love you."

Say "I love you" as much as possible during this week. Tell your children you love them at least once every twenty-four hours. Say "I love you" when you send them off to school, when they come home from school, when you tuck them in at night, anytime, and all the time.

- Write "I love you" on windows and mirrors with lipstick or dry erase markers.
- Leave "I love you" notes inside backpacks, lunch sacks, shoes, pockets, and under pillows.
- Send an email or text message saying, "I love you."

Older children could find this expression of love uncomfortable and think they are too big to love their parents; however, older children need to hear it all the more. Top it off with hugs and kisses.

When your children do something that frustrates you or is against the rules, first say "I love you," followed by what displeased you and how it should be made right.

Don't leave your husband out of this experience. Tell your husband several times that you love him also, making sure your children hear.

When it is your turn to offer the family prayer, also profess your love to deity.

Love at Home

date ....

....
....
....
....
....
....
....
....
....
....
....
....
....
....
....
....
....
....
....
....
....
....
....
....

Self-reliance

*"All of our Church and family actions should be directed
toward making our children and members self-reliant."*

MARION G. ROMNEY

GOAL: Teach your children to be responsible for themselves.

Teaching children to do things for themselves gives them confidence, a
sense of freedom, frees up your time from continual service, and ultimately
helps them grow into happy, competent adults.

To begin this week, make a list of the work you do both for the family
and around the house, that your children can do already or learn to do.
Decide on one or two jobs that you would like to teach *each* child.

Ideas for younger children might include:
+ making their bed
+ picking up clothes
+ pouring a cup of milk
+ making their own sandwich
+ getting ready for bed
+ folding clothes
+ dusting
+ using the vacuum
+ gathering trash
+ washing the dishes
+ cleaning sinks and toilets
+ cleaning mirrors and windows
+ watering plants
+ pulling weeds
+ caring for a pet

In addition to those above, older children could learn chores and
household tasks such as:
+ using appliances
+ mopping
+ shopping
+ cooking a well-balanced meal

- doing laundry following fabric care labels
- mending
- simple home repairs
- hanging a picture
- fixing a running toilet
- lawn maintenance
- basic car maintenance
- pumping gas
- checking oil and fluids
- checking tire pressure
- changing a tire
- jump-starting the car

When you have chosen the jobs you would like your children to learn, plan a time this week to teach them the correct way to do the job. You might consider breaking the job into smaller steps or making a written list of steps to follow.

If your children are capable of doing the job, don't settle for a job half-done or not done to your expectation. Teach them to do it right, and you will both be proud of a job done right the first time. Frequently evaluate what your children have learned and what more you could teach them on their way to being self-reliant.

Self-reliance

date ....

....

....

....

....

....

....

....

....

....

....

....

....

....

....

....

....

....

....

....

....

....

....

Create Work

"Every man and woman and child should work.
Even little children should learn how to share, to help
do the housework and the yardwork . . . . We want
you parents to create work for your children."

THE TEACHINGS OF SPENCER W. KIMBALL

GOAL: Make a list of chores for each child to accomplish each day and guide them in their assignments.

I love the above quote. In following that counsel, and in conjunction with last week's topic, this week the children will be assigned chores to accomplish each day. Make a simple list or a chart with the chores your children are assigned. Provide stickers or another way they can mark their progress and completion of their chores. Be quick to offer encouragement as they work and praise them for their accomplishments.

Make sure the tasks match your children's abilities. Younger children will have simpler tasks than your older children. Obviously, responsibilities increase as the children grow older. Also, take into account children who are already overburdened with school, sports, or other projects; but don't let these be an excuse to skip chores all together.

Set aside a specific time of the day when chores are to be done. For example, chores should be done before they can participate in other activities such as watching TV, playing on the computer, joining friends, getting on the phone, or going outside to play.

It might be hard at first to get children to do chores when they aren't accustom to doing them. Don't make it drudgery; instead, continually praise and encourage. Try your hand at making chores creative and fun. Games such as racing the clock, sock-ball basketball, or treasure hunt pick-up take the "work" out of chores.

Help your children with their chores with the objective of *teaching* them to do it on their own. Make sure you are not coerced into doing their chores for them.

Experience has taught me that children will fib about completing their chores. Thus, chores need to be checked-off by a parent when completed. Make a policy not to accept any excuses for chores not done or only partially done. *Be a stickler and never negotiate—unless you want that to be your never-ending chore!* Be firm and consistent. Add a family rule that if a chore is not fully completed, an additional chore will be added the next day.

If you know your child has honestly done *their best* in completing a chore, it is okay to mark it complete. Resist the temptation to redo a child's chore to a higher level of quality. If one of your children were to see you doing this, he may feel disappointed that his job wasn't up to your standards.

Create Work

date ....

....
....
....
....
....
....
....
....
....
....
....
....
....
....
....
....
....
....
....
....
....
....
....
....

Play Every Day

*"We demonstrate our love for family
members . . . in giving them of our time."*

SUSAN W. TANNER

GOAL: Make a point to really play with your children every day.

In a parenting class my husband and I attended several years ago, sponsored by our church, the only idea that stuck with me these many years later was to "play every day." So, the most important word this week is *play*. Include play in your list of priorities each day. Learn to let go, have fun, not take yourself too seriously, laugh a lot, and *smile*.

+ Take your children to the playground—go down the slide, crawl through the tunnels, scale the monkey bars, or play hide and seek in the trees.
+ Participate in a make-believe tea party, or play school.
+ Be crafty and paint rocks, decorate T-shirts, or make friendship bracelets, sock puppets, or paper snowflakes to hang in your children's bedrooms.
+ Play outside by planning a scavenger hunt, catching fireflies, building a snowman, jumping into rain puddles, or playing in leaf piles, mud, or snow drifts.
+ Explore a local museum.
+ Visit a farm to pick your own fruit and vegetables.
+ Be a sport and play badminton, croquet, horseshoes, hopscotch, four-square, basketball, volleyball, handball, or jump on the trampoline.
+ Go to the beach and jump in the ocean while holding hands and help them build the biggest sand castle ever.
+ Play old-time board games like Monopoly, Chutes and Ladders, Candy Land, or Parchesi. Build a house of cards or make a time capsule.
+ On the weekend, camp out in the family room with sleeping bags, with a fire in the fireplace, movies, s'mores, pillow fights, and ghost stories by flashlight.
+ As you play informally and are more fun-loving around the house,

your children will want you to be involved in their life and will think, "You're the coolest, Mom!"

Play Every Day

date ....

....
....
....
....
....
....
....
....
....
....
....
....
....
....
....
....
....
....
....
....
....
....
....

Pray Always

*"In the past, having family prayer once a day may
have been all right. But in the future it will not be
enough if we are going to save our families."*

SPENCER W. KIMBALL (*as quoted by* JAMES E. FAUST)

GOAL: Make prayer a priority for you and your family.

We are admonished to "pray in your families unto the Father, always in my name, that your wives and your children may be blessed" (3 Nephi 18:21). Prayer is a wonderful resource to help us through our sojourn here on earth. If we can teach this concept to our children at an early age, how much easier and fulfilling their lives will be.

Start this week on a spiritual note with an FHE lesson on the topic of prayer, referring to the ideas in the FHE Resource Book.[1] Also, this week:

+ Talk with your children about all the things they can and should pray for.
+ Make a picture chart for younger children to remember while they are praying.
+ Say prayers together in the morning before everyone leaves.
+ Make sure prayers are said over all meals.
+ Say evening prayer together as a family.
+ Kneel with each child beside their bed as they learn to say their personal prayers before going to bed.
+ Get in the mind-set of encouraging your children to seek answers from their Heavenly Father when they have a decision to make.

Instruct your children to use the sacred pronouns of *thee, thou, thy,* and *thine* during their prayers to show greater respect to deity.

Be certain to say your own prayers, both morning and evening, and in between. Let your children see you on your knees in personal prayer.

Strive to have a prayer in your heart at all times, wherever you are or whatever you are doing. Notice what a difference having increased prayer in your life and the lives of your family makes.

Notes:
1. *FHE Resource Book*, Lesson 7, "Heavenly Father Answers Our Prayers," 27; or Lesson 18, "Unity Through Family Prayer," 80.

Pray Always

date ....

....

....

....

....

....

....

....

....

....

....

....

....

....

....

....

....

....

....

....

....

....

....

....

TWELVE

Ask for Good Behavior

"It is in the home that our behavior is most significant. It is the place where our actions have the greatest impact, for good or ill."

WAYNE S. PETERSON

GOAL: Ask for and expect the behavior you want from your children.

Research shows that children learn more from positive interactions rather than negative ones. So this week you are going to practice a method of correcting your children that eliminates the negative aspect.

Instead of telling your children what "not to do," tell them what you want them "to do." For example, instead of saying, "Don't put your feet on the furniture," say "Feet on the floor, please." Rather than saying, "Don't talk with your mouth full," say "Talk to me after you have chewed and swallowed your food."

More examples include:

+ "Please talk quietly in the house."
+ "I would appreciate it if you used your indoor voice."
+ "Please clean up the bathroom when you are done."
+ "The bus is leaving soon—please be on time."

This is a very easy parenting technique to grasp and put into action. It makes you feel more in control of situations and that you're not continually rebuking your children. You will also see an immediate change in your children's behavior.

Ask for Good Behavior

date ....

....
....
....
....
....
....
....
....
....
....
....
....
....
....
....
....
....
....
....
....
....
....
....
....

Turn Off

*"We should strive to change the corrupt and immoral
tendencies in television and in society by keeping
things that offend and debase out of our homes."*

M. RUSSELL BALLARD

GOAL: Turn off or limit the television, computer games, videos, the Internet, and other electronic gadgets.

The influence of electronic entertainment is a major factor in family dynamics, be it for good or bad. Statistics *overwhelmingly* show that excessive media has negative effects on our children. Television has a tremendous influence on its young viewers—probably far more than we will ever realize. This is not only from the behavior it produces, but the behavior it prevents—time wasted in not pursuing other interests. It is worthwhile to note that research has shown two hours of daily television viewing was acceptable, but beyond that time the negative effects on children multiplied.

To make this week successful, it is essential that you start with a family meeting to inform everyone what you will be doing and why. Suggestions can be found in the *Family Home Evening Resource Book.*[1] Make sure the family is aware that they are not being punished, but that you want to experience home life without the influence of television and other electronics. During the family meeting make a list of activities to do instead of watching television, playing video games, and so forth.

If your family is not ready to go cold turkey just yet, consider:
+ limiting the amount of time they spend watching TV
+ restricting the source (such as just the television)
+ limiting what your children watch to certain channels or shows
+ limiting electronics on school nights
+ declaring one night a "TV-free night"
+ require children to spend equal amounts of time doing other indoor or outdoor activities as they spend with electronics
+ experimenting for one or two days with restrictions, or for only certain hours of the day

To counter the problems associated with television viewing, families need to establish rules and guidelines (in your Family Rule Book) to limit how much time is spent absorbed in the television, computer, and electronic games. Make sure you specify that chores and homework must be completed before watching television and that dinner will be eaten with the television off.

Always know what your children are viewing or listening to. Discuss with them if the subjects addressed are contrary to the gospel, and teach them how to apply gospel principles in choosing appropriate media.

Getting your children to comply when it's time to turn off the computer or television can be very frustrating. There are devices and software that automatically limit their access time. Search out these options until you find what works best to help shield your family from these outside influences.

> *Your efforts in this area will most likely be met with resistance, rebellion, and even revolt. Be prepared to stand your ground. Also, be keenly aware if your child is intentionally "escaping" to a friend's house or elsewhere to gain access to what is no longer available at home.*

Notes:
1.   *FHE Resource Book,* Lesson Idea, "Media," 207–208.

Turn Off

date ....

....
....
....
....
....
....
....
....
....
....
....
....
....
....
....
....
....
....
....
....
....
....
....
....
....

Loving Touch

" 'Have you hugged your child today?' How fortunate, how
blessed is the child who feels the affection of his parents. That
warmth, that love will bear sweet fruit in the years that follow."

GORDON B. HINCKLEY

GOAL: Give your children extra *physical* affection and attention.

Have you ever experienced a big bear hug that fully encompassed you with love? Has someone you highly admired ever patted you on the back? Do you remember your dad tickling the bottoms of your feet when you were little, while you laughed hysterically and squirmed to get away? These small and simple acts made you feel closer to that person, raised your self-esteem, and made you *feel* loved.

Throughout this week let your children *feel* love.

- Give your children a big hug or a squeeze for no reason.
- Pat your children on the back.
- Give your children high fives.
- Steal a kiss on your children's checks when they least expect it.
- Purposefully sit next to your children and put your arm around them.
- Lightly tickle their arm.
- Hold their hand for a moment.
- Squeeze their knee.
- Give a quick back rub.
- Lie down next to them to watch television.
- Evolve into a kissing or a tickle "monster" and chase your children around the house.

When your children leave and return to the house each day, give them a hug and a kiss. If they don't willingly return your hugs and kisses, then ask for them.

You'll be surprised how easy it becomes for your children to return that same love back to you.

Loving Touch

date ....

....

....

....

....

....

....

....

....

....

....

....

....

....

....

....

....

....

....

....

....

....

....

....

....

FIFTEEN

Dinnertime

*"Mealtime provides a wonderful time to review
the activities of the day and to not only feed
the body, but to feed the spirit as well."*

EZRA TAFT BENSON

GOAL: Have a home-cooked dinner together every night as a family and make it a time to "feed the spirit" as well.

Having dinner as a family may be the *most powerful* and *most underused* tool you have for drawing your family closer together. Research has proven that children who have meals together with their family have fewer problems overall than those children in families who do not make the time for this simple act.

This week, plan every evening's meal in advance. Planning will ensure there will be no last-minute panic with an opt-out for fast food. Make food that the family enjoys and create a "coming together and sharing time." Try to have all family members present at the table. Inevitably someone will have a practice to be at, a meeting to attend or be running late, but try to have the majority of the family present.

Be creative and make dinnertime fun:

- Set the table with a tablecloth, centerpiece, fancy napkins, and your special dinnerware.
- If the weather is good, spread a blanket on the back lawn and have a picnic—if not, have an indoor picnic in the family room.
- Roast hot dogs and marshmallows in your fireplace.
- Have dinner on the front porch.
- Serve breakfast for dinner and have everyone wear pajamas to the table.
- Eat with chopsticks.
- Let your child be "chef for the day." Let him choose the meal and help with all the preparation.
- Play musical chairs by rotating seating positions so each child will have a turn at the head of the dinner table.
- During the meal ask family members to share what the best thing was that happened to them that day. Ask everyone what their

funniest moment of the day was, or what great things they did that day. See if they did something kind during the day they'd like to share with everyone.

Consider making a "conversation jar" with conversation ideas or questions written on strips of paper inside. Each night at the dinner table, one family member pulls out one strip of paper and reads it to the family. Family members then take turns talking about the topic or question. This is a great way to have family discussions on spiritual topics.

Another fun addition for mealtimes is to have a special plate that alternates between family members or is set for a child who deserves special recognition. Whoever has the special plate gets to have the other family members say special things about him.

If you have children who have picky appetites and don't care for what is being served, you shouldn't necessarily offer to prepare something else. Instead, insist they try at least a certain portion, or number of bites of what has been prepared. They can then *prepare for themselves* something additional to eat. It is not necessary to cater to everyone's palate

Emphasize that manners are required when eating with the family. Do not allow bickering, fighting, or other behavior that would detract from the togetherness you are working to develop. You might need to add dinnertime rules to the Family Rule Book.

Do your best to make dinner a coming-together time the entire family can look forward to—a place where they can share, participate, and invite the Spirit to dwell.

Dinnertime

date ....

....
....
....
....
....
....
....
....
....
....
....
....
....
....
....
....
....
....
....
....
....
....

SIXTEEN

Provide Choices

"Teach children how to make their own decisions, even
if it involves their failing once in a while. We need to
help children come to an understanding such as Lehi
taught, 'knowing good from evil; to act for themselves
and not to be acted upon' (2 Nephi 2:26)."

BEN R. BANKS

GOAL: Give your children choices this week (make sure they are choices you can live with).

Once rules in a home are established, children then have the *choice* to obey the rules or not. Learning how to make choices, especially *correct* choices, is a very important life skill. Once children learn that *their* choices are important and make a difference, only then can they learn how to make the *right* choices.

Thus, this week you are going to increase your children's opportunities to make choices. Consider starting the week with an FHE lesson that includes role play.[1] Then you can discuss the consequences of good choices versus bad choices.

When the need to make a decision arises, provide your children two or three options. You want them to practice thinking about their options and consequences, but do not want them to be overwhelmed. Younger children can be given simple choices, and older children can be trusted with weightier ones.

Give choices such as:
+ Would you like waffles, pancakes or French toast for breakfast?
+ Would you prefer to wear the blue long-sleeved shirt or the green short-sleeved shirt? (Let them know what the weather will be like that day.)
+ Which of your chores would you like to do first?
+ Would you like to watch television or go outside and throw a ball?
+ What gift did you think we should buy Abigail for her birthday party?

As you go throughout your day, notice how many choices you make on behalf of your children. Allow your children to make as many of these choices as appropriate and possible.

If your children make a good decision, praise them. If they make a choice that isn't necessarily the right one, that's okay too. Don't try to talk them out of their decision. Have your children follow-through with their choice and allow them to learn from it. After they have made an incorrect choice, consequences need to follow. Then talk with them about how they could have made a better choice and come up with a different resolution for next time.

Notes:
1.   *FHE Resource Book*, Lesson 8, "We Can Choose," 31.

Provide Choices

....
....
....
....
....
....
....
....
....
....
....
....
....
....
....
....
....
....
....
....
....
....
....
....

SEVENTEEN

Avoiding Interruptions

*"I should be allowed to continue the work of
translation without interruption."*

JOSEPH SMITH—HISTORY 1:75

GOAL: Identify when your children (and you) are inappropriately interrupting others and apply techniques to correct this behavior.

Scores of people (not just children) have developed such a bad habit of interrupting others that they have become entirely unaware when they are doing so.

My neighbor has a kinder, gentler way of addressing these interruptions with her girls. When she is in a conversation with someone else, and one of her daughters attempts to interrupt her, she holds up her finger (as if to signal "one") toward her daughter, never drawing attention away from the person with whom she is speaking. She keeps her finger in the air, directed at her daughter, until she is *completely* done with her conversation, and then diverts her attention toward her daughter.

This method satisfies both the mom (because she is able to carry on her conversation) and her daughters (because they knew they will get their mom's attention next).

Pay close attention this week to occasions when your children interrupt your conversations and apply the "one-finger method" used by my neighbor. Also, take notice if you are guilty of interrupting and take appropriate steps to show greater courtesy.

Avoiding Interruptions

date ....

....

....

....

....

....

....

....

....

....

....

....

....

....

....

....

....

....

....

....

....

....

....

....

....

Scripture Power

*"I feel certain that if, in our homes, parents will read from
the Book of Mormon prayerfully and regularly, both by
themselves and with their children, the spirit of that great
book will come to permeate our homes. . . . The spirit of
reverence will increase; mutual respect and consideration for
each other will grow. The spirit of contention will depart. . . .
Righteousness will increase. Faith, hope, and charity . . .
will abound . . . bringing . . . peace, joy and happiness."*

M A R I O N   G .   R O M N E Y

GOAL: Seek to have the power of the Book of Mormon in your home by
having daily scripture study.

Modern-day prophets have said that the scriptures are "the words of
life" and the Book of Mormon specifically contains a power that "will begin
to flow into your lives the moment you begin a serious study of the book.
You will find greater power to resist temptation. You will find the power to
avoid deception. You will find the power to stay on the strait and narrow
path."[1] Nowhere else have such profound promises been made about
keeping your family and yourself on the right path. Why would anyone
not want these blessings in their lives?

To get your children excited about studying the scriptures, consider
sharing the lesson on studying the scriptures together from the FHE
Resource Book.[2]

To be successful, it is imperative that you set a specific time that the
family gathers for scripture study every day. If you're just beginning, it's a
good idea to set a daily alarm as a reminder, so the time doesn't slip away.
Place your scriptures in a visible location, at or near the place where you
will study together, so you have a visual reminder and it is easy to begin
once you gather.

For small children, you could adapt the scriptures to their level of
understanding by using simplified scriptures or pictures from the Gospel
Art Packet (also available from the Church Distribution Center). To help
teach, add interest, and make the scriptures more meaningful, discuss
what you read and liken the situations and challenges to your own family's

situations and challenges.

You should also schedule a time for yourself to indulge in personal scripture study. It is important to pray before you begin your studies and have a pen and paper at hand to make note of the thoughts and impressions that come to your mind.

As we know too well, children learn by example. What better way is there to teach this principle than by letting your children see you in personal scripture study? Let them see you reading when they get up in the morning or when they come home from school. Let them see you engage in scripture study on the Sabbath or whenever there is quiet time.

Notes:
1. Ezra Taft Benson, "The Keystone to Our Religion," *Ensign*, Jan. 1992, 17.
2. *FHE Resource Book*, Lesson 4, "Studying the Scriptures Together," 17.

Scripture Power

date ....

....
....
....
....
....
....
....
....
....
....
....
....
....
....
....
....
....
....
....
....
....
....
....
....

Listen with Love

"Listen to your child . . . with all of you. . . . Listen
patiently to the end, until he has emptied his heart.
Encourage him, looking directly in his eyes, . . .
Listen, and savor the joy of having this child."

WINNIFRED C. JARDINE

GOAL: Take the time to listen to your children, and try to understand what they are *feeling* as well as what they are *saying*.

A lot has been written on the fine art of listening. There are numerous techniques you could try; the steps below are just some of the basics. The most important part of listening is to be attentive so your children know you *want* to listen, making them feel important, worthwhile, and loved.

While listening to each child:

1. Look in his eyes. Get down on his level (if needed).
2. *Smile.*
3. Pay attention and try to understand what he is feeling, as well as what he is saying.
4. Do not be quick to respond. Wait a few moments to make sure your child is completely done talking before you reply.
5. Respond without criticizing. Avoid sarcastic, light-hearted joking, or angry responses. Be mindful of fluctuated tones in your voice, indifferent facial expressions, sighs or groans, and shrugging of shoulders. *Respond only with love.*

Listening to older children and teenagers is a bit more complex. In addition to the guidance above, consider the following when communicating with teenagers:

1. Be available to listen. This is the *most important* of these guidelines. Most teenagers don't like to talk when siblings are around, so find time to be with them one-on-one. Try engaging them in an activity that isn't too distracting such as going on a walk, playing catch, or doing a light chore together. Often teens seem to be more talkative at night. Be willing to stay up for a late-night chat if necessary.
2. Some teenagers find face-to-face encounters to be confrontational. Sitting or standing side-by-side can be very advantageous.

3. Allow extra time before responding. Teens need time to sort through their feelings and formulate their thoughts. Give them time to think before you respond.
4. Don't talk too much. Ask if they would like to hear your advice or know what you think.
5. Ask open ended questions to keep the communication flowing.
6. When children feel like they can freely talk and that their parents really *want* to listen, a strong bond is established that can endure throughout the years.

Listen with Love

date ....

....
....
....
....
....
....
....
....
....
....
....
....
....
....
....
....
....
....
....
....
....
....
....
....

Worthy Music

"Music has boundless powers for moving families toward greater spirituality and devotion to the gospel. Latter-day Saints should fill their homes with the sound of worthy music."

GOAL: Fill your home with gentle, uplifting, and worthy music as much as possible.

Although I skipped parenting classes and music classes in the premortal world, I have come to appreciate how good music can help invite the Spirit into our homes and help us grow closer to our Father in Heaven. People of all ages are influenced by good music as it can spur creativity, lift our spirits, and deepen our faith.

The First Presidency has admonished us to teach our children to love the hymns and has added that the "hymns can help us withstand the temptations."[1] If you don't already have uplifting music available in your home, ask friends and family for recommendations. Carefully choose music that will elevate and inspire. Make sure to include the hymns in your selection.

Kick off this topic with a family home evening lesson. *The Family Home Evening Resource Book* has lesson ideas on music.[2]

During the week, try waking up to the music you have selected. Listen while working and playing, and while in the car. Have gentle music playing as your children come home from school, and play Sabbath-appropriate music on Sunday mornings as everyone gets ready for church. Sing the hymns and primary songs in family home evening, before scripture study and prayer times, and encourage your children to sing along.

Pay attention to your children's response to the influence of worthy music. Watch for the results of peace, tranquility, patience, and family members showing greater love toward one another.

Notes:
1. "First Presidency Preface to the Hymns," *Hymns*, x.
2. *FHE Resource Book*, Lesson Ideas, "Music," 212–213.

Worthy Music

date ....

....
....
....
....
....
....
....
....
....
....
....
....
....
....
....
....
....
....
....
....
....
....
....
....
....

A House of Order

*"Organize yourselves; prepare every needful
thing; and establish . . . a house of order"*

D&C 88:119

GOAL: Help your children establish a place for everything and schedule a
time for daily cleanup.

One of the skills you want your children to develop is to bring order
to their lives. This involves establishing a place for belongings, returning
items to their correct place, and knowing when to dispose of items when
no longer needed. Effectively teaching this skill might require some
improvement on your part, so this can truly be a family effort.

This week, help your children organize and maintain their belongings.
Start in the bedroom. Decide on specific places for all of their toys, books,
clothes, and other belongings. Label boxes or containers if needed to help
your children keep things organized.

One of my children just cannot keep his toys and belongings organized
despite every technique we have tried. I finally bought him two big red
buckets to keep in his closet or a corner of his room. When it is time to
clean up, all of his toys and everything on the floor of his bedroom gets
dumped into the buckets. If he particularly cares for an item, he is expected
to find a safe place for it where it won't get tossed into the buckets with
everything else.

As you help your children organize during the week, be sure to pull out
toys, clothes, and other belongings they no longer use or have outgrown.
Either donate or discard these old items.

Outside of their bedrooms, backpacks, library books, lunch boxes,
unfinished homework, coats, dirty clothes, sports equipment, wet bath
towels, and so forth, should all have their designated places. Unless
another place is established, all toys and belongings should be returned to
the children's rooms when they are done playing.

It is important that after a place has been established for all items, a
pick-up routine of at least five minutes be scheduled every day. This will
help your children keep their belongings in place and their rooms clutter-
free. A good time for clean-up is prior to bedtime; however, your children

may be too grumpy or tired to help, so you may need to schedule it earlier in the day.

When toys or belongings are left out overnight at my house, they go into "toy jail." If my children want something out of toy jail, they are required to do an extra chore. Having to do a "cleaning" chore works well as a natural consequence of not cleaning up earlier.

A House of Order

date ....

....
....
....
....
....
....
....
....
....
....
....
....
....
....
....
....
....
....
....
....
....
....

Just Say "Yes"

"But I say, Have they not heard? Yes verily, their sound went into all the earth, and their words unto the ends of the world."

ROMANS 10:18

GOAL: This week you are only allowed to say "yes."

As a parent, your job is to guide and direct your children. More often than not, what children ask for is not in their best interest at that time. Thus your most recurrent word is *no*. However, this week we are going to stir things up a bit. You are going to practice saying "no" by actually saying "yes."

This doesn't mean that you will be a pushover or that your children will get whatever they want. It means that you are going to answer their every request beginning with a "yes." You will be learning to give a negative response with an affirmative answer.

When your children start to ask you a question, resolve in your mind that the first word of your answer will be "yes" and then determine how to phrase the rest of the sentence to answer appropriately.

Because we all need a little help, here are some ideas:

+ "Yes, we can put a puzzle together."
+ "Yes, we can go to a movie another night."
+ "Yes, you can have cookies as soon as you eat this apple."
+ "Yes, we can have brownies for dessert if you make them."
+ "Yes, James can sleep over when your dad and I can determine a good time."
+ "Yes, you can have a pony . . . when you are older and leave home."

Try to be creative in how you say "no" by saying "yes." Think of it as a challenge to toy with your child's brain without them knowing it.

This week might be a struggle as you will need to come up with creative answers, but it should be interesting to see how your children respond to their "new parent."

Just Say "Yes"

date ....

....
....
....
....
....
....
....
....
....
....
....
....
....
....
....
....
....
....
....
....
....
....
....
....

Reconnect at the Crossroads

*"Take time to always be at the crossroads in the lives
of your children, whether they be six or sixteen."*

EZRA TAFT BENSON

(*as quoted by* THOMAS S. MONSON)

GOAL: Be there when your children come through the door, and spend ten
to fifteen minutes of dedicated time focusing on *each* child.

In today's world, with working parents and extra-curricular activities
for children, parents and children need to have a reconnecting time—a
time when you focus on each child, giving them your undivided attention.
This reconnecting time tells your children you missed them, you care for
them, and you want to know how they are doing.

As your children come through the door this week, be there to greet
them and ask how their day went. Ask your children who they sat with at
lunch, who they played with at recess, what kind of homework they have,
and ask if they need any help.

If you cannot be home when your children come through the door,
leave a note or make a phone call. This will give them a sense of security,
knowing that someone cares and is looking out for them. It will also give
you peace of mind knowing that your children are home safely. Be sure
that when *you* come home and walk through the door that you spend a few
minutes focusing on *each* child. Seek out each child if needed and spend
some time playing with him, listening to his thoughts and his account of
the day's events. It doesn't have to be a long time, just enough to show that
you care.

When you greet your children, make an effort to be cheerful, to *smile*,
and show them how happy you are to see them. Do not listen to phone
messages or review the mail until you have reconnected with each child.

Even if your children are working, dating, or stay out late, make an
effort to be there when they come home and spend a few minutes talking
with them. If you fall asleep before they get home, instruct them to wake
you when they arrive.

Reconnect at the Crossroads

date ....

....

....

....

....

....

....

....

....

....

....

....

....

....

....

....

....

....

....

....

....

....

....

....

TWENTY-FOUR

Sibling Rivalry

*"[Satan] damages and often destroys families
within the walls of their own homes. His strategy
is to stir up anger between family members."*

LYNN G. ROBBINS

GOAL: Tolerate no fighting or quarreling.

Subduing sibling rivalry is definitely one of those important lessons I missed when skipping the parenting classes I referred to in the beginning. I struggle every day with how to handle it as a parent. With three very active boys and one strong-willed girl, it seems they are continually picking on each other, defending attacks, or collapsing on the floor in defeat.

Let me assure you that sibling rivalry is a natural family "disease." That said, not all sibling rivalry is bad; but it needs to be *carefully* monitored to avoid spiritual or emotional damage to any one particular child.

There is no guaranteed method that will rid your home of this plague. All I can offer are suggestions for you to choose from, and hope that one or more will be successful in your family. To bring this matter to your family's attention you should consider starting the week with an FHE lesson that addresses this matter.[1] The following are ideas from which to choose and apply this week in an effort to subdue sibling rivalry.

1. *Ignore the fighting.* Whenever your children start quarreling, simply ignore them. Pretend you don't notice what they are doing. If it gets too difficult to ignore, get up and walk into another room or go outside. The only time a parent is allowed to intervene is if physical injury is imminent or has occurred. Allegedly, if parents stay out of the squabbles, children will learn to work out their own problems and eventually get along. This also teaches your children how to deal with adversity on their own.

2. *Send them elsewhere.* Tell the participants if they want to continue fighting they are free to do so, but they must go to another room, the backyard, or somewhere else where they will not disturb the peace and spirit of your home. This usually ends their squabble quickly as their audience is taken away.

3. *Separate the contenders.* Send them to their rooms. If they share a

room, then send one to their room and the other to the time-out chair. Instruct them to stay there until they are ready to apologize to each other and peacefully resolve whatever problem started it all.

4. *Give more chores.* A good philosophy is that if your children are fighting, they have too much time on their hands; they could use that time instead to perform additional chores.

5. *Write it down.* If your children are old enough, have the participants sit down and write their complaints about the other child and the circumstances. This not only improves their writing ability, but gets them to think rationally about what happened and whether it could have been dealt with in another manner.

6. *Keep score.* When my children keep feeding off each other and won't stop fighting, I write their names on the kitchen whiteboard. I then inform them that whoever continues to fight will get a mark under their name for every offense. When they ask me what kind of punishment will be given to the child with the most marks, I just say, "We'll have to wait and see." Oddly enough, the bickering ends rather quickly, and I have never had to enforce any kind of punishment.

7. *Praise them.* When you observe your children being kind and productively working together (rather than bickering and fighting), praise them.

8. *Pray.* When all else fails, ask for higher guidance to your *specific* challenges.

Notes:
1. *FHE Resource Book,* Lesson 21, "Family Unite," 92; or Lesson Ideas, "Contention," 180–181.

Sibling Rivalry

date ....

....
....
....
....
....
....
....
....
....
....
....
....
....
....
....
....
....
....
....
....
....
....
....
....
....

TWENTY-FIVE

Unseen Visitor

*"I believe when a woman chooses to have Christ
at the center of her own heart . . . she brings the
Lord into the core of her home and family."*

ANNE C. PINGREE

GOAL: Conduct yourself as if Christ were a visitor in your home this week.

This week can be very effective and have a long-lasting impression if done correctly. Commence this week with a family home evening focusing on Christ and how He is always watching us. During FHE, ask the children how they would act differently if Christ were in your home.[1] Give real-life scenarios, using examples from your own family and ask how they might treat each other differently if Christ were there.

Put a picture of Christ where it can readily be seen as a reminder. If you already have a picture of Christ in your home, move it to a different location so your family will pay greater attention to it. You could even purchase a picture of Christ for each child to hang in his room.

During the week when your children do something that is not acceptable, ask them if they would have done that if Christ were there watching them. Ask them in a teaching and loving manner, careful not to accuse or criticize.

Apply this theory to your own parenting practices. If Christ were in your home, watching your mothering technique, would you act differently? Would you be slower to anger? Would you keep your house a bit tidier? Would you be more thoughtful and try a little harder?

Notes:

1. *FHE Resource Book*, Lesson 12, "Jesus is my Example," 49; or Lesson 17, "Love at Home," 74.

Unseen Visitor

date ....

....
....
....
....
....
....
....
....
....
....
....
....
....
....
....
....
....
....
....
....
....
....
....
....
....

Surprise, Surprise!

*"To many, the announcement came as a
surprise, a very welcome surprise."*

BOYD K. PACKER

GOAL: Do something out of character to surprise and make your children feel special.

Do your children think you're a stick in the mud? That you're all business and no fun? Show them your fun side this week. Make a plan of fun things you can do with and for your children. (Okay, so it's not really spontaneous if you have to plan it, but for some, this challenge gives us the incentive to introduce our children to the parent they have never known.)

Ideas to consider:

- Go out for an ice cream sundae in place of dinner.
- Stop at a park while running errands and let your children try out every piece of equipment at the playground.
- Do one of their chores "just because" or declare a "no chore day."
- Leave notes or small gifts where other family members can find them (make sure you leave one for your husband also).
- Announce double-dessert night.
- Roll down a grassy hill with your children because it has always looked fun.
- Drive them to get ice cream in their pajamas.
- Drop some letters in the mail for your children as getting mail is always a special event.
- Organize a secret treasure hunt. Make a map or a series of clues that will lead your child from one room to the next. The treasure could be a special treat such as a book, a toy, or an IOU for a special trip out.

Some really "fun" moms take their child out of school one day a year to hang out together, play games, watch movies, or bake cookies.

Transform yourself into a fun mom this week, and remember to *smile* while you are doing it.

Surprise, Surprise!

date

TWENTY-SEVEN

Be Responsible

"Children need to learn responsibility and independence."

JAMES E. FAUST

GOAL: Teach your children the basic responsibility of cleaning up after themselves.

I had a college roommate who was raised with hired "house-help" her entire life and did not know how to clean or to pick up after herself. She left her belongings strewn all over the apartment, which was a great source of frustration to the rest of her roommates. I clearly recall the day she made herself a sandwich and left peanut butter and jelly droppings all over the kitchen counter and floor. She was oblivious to the fact that it was *her* responsibility to clean up the mess.

None of us want our children to be like this. Children need to accept responsibility and clean up after themselves, not just for others, but for their own dignity and peace of mind. Even very young children can, and should, learn to clean up after themselves.

Begin this week with a FHE lesson addressing this topic.[1] This will set the tone for the week and will make it easier when you insist that your children clean and pick up after themselves.

Teach your children to put away whatever they use, whether it is theirs, yours, or someone else's. For example, if your children borrow the scissors and tape for a project, make sure they know to put the items back so they can be found the next time.

Have your children clear their own dishes from the table, and, if possible, put them in the dishwasher or sink, ready to be washed. If something is spilled, insist they wipe it up. If your children kick off their shoes or throw their clothes or backpack in the middle of the floor, gently remind them to pick the items up and put them where they belong.

Before bedtime, all family members should go through the house collecting belongings and putting them away—thus reinforcing the five-minute pick-up routine suggested in chapter 21.

Notes:
1. *FHE Resource Book*, Lesson 20, "A House of Order," 89–91.

Be Responsible

date

TWENTY-EIGHT

Cultivate Compassion

"When we have compassion, we open ourselves to feel with others their sorrows and joys."

COMPASSION: FEELING AND ACTING

GOAL: Develop compassion in yourself and your children.

Sometimes as parents we become worn out and numb from the same challenges day after day; and although we truly love our children, we don't necessarily *feel* what our children are feeling, and we ultimately lose perspective or don't understand our children's point of view.

This week, your goal is to cultivate compassion for your children by putting yourself in their shoes, to experience how they feel in different situations. Starting the week with an FHE lesson will broaden your understanding of this subject and will help bring your children onboard with practicing compassion also.[1]

When good or bad situations arise throughout the week, ask yourself, "How would I feel if I were in my children's shoes? How would I want to be treated?" If your children are involved in a situation, talk them through being in the other person's shoes, how they would feel, and want to be treated.

Once you and your children have realized how the other individual is feeling, determine what can be done to help that person feel better, *and then do it.* True compassion culminates in action.

By developing and practicing compassion for others and understanding how others truly feel, we learn Christlike love for *all* people. This is an important element in having a happy home.

As you progress throughout this week, evaluate whether increased compassion changes the atmosphere in your home and if it has a positive affect on your children.

Notes:
1.   *FHE Resource Book,* Lesson 25, "Developing Compassion," 106.

Cultivate Compassion

date ....

....
....
....
....
....
....
....
....
....
....
....
....
....
....
....
....
....
....
....
....
....
....
....
....
....

TWENTY-NINE

Brand-name Labels

"Our lives are guided in large measure by our perceptions."

GORDON B. HINCKLEY

GOAL: Give your children "labels" of encouragement and praise.

Almost every expert on child development tells us that our children will become whatever we tell them they will. We also have been told that children reflect positive behavior when reinforced by a positive environment. Therefore, we should be very careful about the words we use to identify and describe our children.

Throughout this week you are to "label" your children with terms of encouragement and praise. Tell them they are:

- wonderful
- kind
- clean
- brilliant
- fantastic
- outstanding
- splendid
- awesome
- funny
- talented
- gifted
- clever

- smart
- honest
- magnificent
- great
- amazing
- superb
- tremendous
- out of this world
- incredible
- skillful
- exceptional

Try to smother them in as many ooey-gooey adjectives as possible. You could even create superhero names for your children!

A fun practice is to name your child's favorite dish after them, such as "Matt"aroni-n-Cheese; or even their favorite drinks: Trent's Apple Bubbly (sparkling cider), or Katelyn's "CM" (chocolate milk). Make sure you serve these specially labeled dishes and drinks on their birthdays, special events, or anytime they need a pick-me-up.

When this week is over your children will probably have a spring in their step and smiles on their faces from remembering all the wonderful words you have said about them.

Brand-name Labels

date ....

....
....
....
....
....
....
....
....
....
....
....
....
....
....
....
....
....
....
....
....
....
....
....
....
....
....

Tones of Love

"Christlike communications are expressed in
tones of love rather than loudness"

L. LIONEL KENDRICK

GOAL: Speak softly, calmly, and with greater love.

Yelling, shouting, and screaming are surefire ways to drive the Spirit away from our homes. I remorsefully admit that I am guilty of this offense. I notice that I tend to get louder when I am engulfed in stress, or when I am worn down from refereeing the same skirmish day in and day out.

Have you ever known some children to yell, shout, or scream as part of their ordinary speaking voice? These children do not know how to talk without being overbearing and loud. They come from an environment where they need to talk loud in order to be heard over the competing noises in their home and of family members. *The ideal home should be a quiet, peaceful place where the Spirit feels comfortable and wants to stay.*

This week, try to keep your voice at a low, soothing level. Try not to yell or raise your voice, but speak with greater kindness and love. Make it a practice (or even a rule) not to yell across the house. Take time to consider both the volume *and* tone of voice used within your home. Ask yourself, "Am I loud?" or "Am I sharp, abrupt, angry, or judgmental?" If you need to reprimand a child, remember to do so in soft tones, or even try to whisper your directives. The scriptures teach us that "a soft answer turneth away wrath: but grievous words stir up anger" (Proverbs 15:1).

Get your children in on this "game" and declare an hour of whispering each day, or play the "whispering game." If your children are arguing, tell them to whisper their disputations. Initiate the "indoor voices" rule, and add this to your Family Rule Book if needed.

Pay particular attention to your children's reaction to your softer speech this week. Do they pay better attention, fight less, or speak softer as a result? Do you notice a more peaceful atmosphere? Do you notice an atmosphere where the Spirit would want to dwell?

Tones of Love

date ....

....
....
....
....
....
....
....
....
....
....
....
....
....
....
....
....
....
....
....
....
....
....
....
....
....

THIRTY ONE

Family Council

*"There are priceless blessings to be obtained from
counseling together with our families, showing a genuine
interest in the lives of our family members."*

ROBERT D. HALES

GOAL: Hold a family council to resolve a problem or to discuss family
business.

When all family members are involved in solving a problem, they learn
the valuable lesson of being on the same team and working together. Over
time, this "team" mentality secures family bonds.

Despite common belief "there is a difference between family home
evening and family council. . . . When family members gather each Monday
evening to learn the gospel, to enjoy one another, and to have fun together,
that is a family home evening. . . . When family members gather to make
important decisions, to recognize the achievements of members of the
family, to discipline, or to plan events, that is a family council."[1]

Many families choose to combine these two distinct meetings; however,
I strongly recommend that these be conducted separately. The risk is too
high that these meetings could detract from one another, especially if a
particularly contentious topic must be addressed during family council.

This week you need to identify an issue, challenge, or opportunity you
would like to discuss and resolve with the family. Work in partnership
with your husband so he can be supportive and possibly conduct and lead
the meeting.

Pick a time and place where the family can gather to hold the family
council. Make sure each family member is aware of the time, the place, and
what you will be discussing so they can prepare their own ideas.

Depending on the nature of the meeting, you may want to start
with a prayer. Begin by describing the problem in an objective way that
encourages constructive participation. Be careful not to place blame. Then
open the meeting for sharing of feelings and ideas on how best to resolve
the problem. Allow each family member to talk without being interrupted
or subjected to impolite words or gestures. Make sure everyone is allowed
to speak and is respectfully listened to. After all discussion has taken place,

work to build consensus toward the most positive resolution.

After a conclusion has been reached, write down the outcome and how the problem will be resolved, and then post this in a conspicuous spot. If it is an issue of rules or discipline, it is best to be included in your Family Rule Book.

By demonstrating to your children how to discuss issues and resolve disagreements in this peaceful manner, they learn important life skills in dealing with future disputes at home or elsewhere in their life.

Notes:
1.   Gardner, Marvin K., "Family Councils: Making Decisions Together," *Ensign*, June 1977, 4.

Family Council

date ....

....
....
....
....
....
....
....
....
....
....
....
....
....
....
....
....
....
....
....
....
....
....
....

Righteous Traditions

"If we build righteous traditions in our families, the
light of the gospel can grow ever brighter in the lives
of our children from generation to generation."

L . T O M   P E R R Y

GOAL: Evaluate your family traditions and determine whether you should
add, modify, continue, or remove certain ones.

I love the quote by L. Tom Perry given above. Never before had I
appreciated how important traditions are, and what a positive influence
they can be to our children and our families. Just as the dynamics of each
family are vastly diverse, so are the traditions of each family. However,
most family traditions are associated with, or geared around, the holidays
and are passed down from generation to generation.

You need to carefully choose the traditions you want to observe in
your own family. Keep in mind that some families go overboard with their
traditions to the point where some family members would rather have a
painful root canal than attend another family event.

To help in evaluating your family traditions, first divide a paper into
two columns. In the first column write all the family traditions your family
participates in. These could include:

+ traditional holidays
+ special occasions—blessing of children, baptisms, ordinations to
  the priesthood, anniversaries, birthdays, and so forth
+ how you conduct family dinnertime
+ special bedtime routine
+ special handshakes or sayings
+ a unique kiss
+ nicknames or pet names for each other
+ girls' week at the beach
+ boys' annual fishing trip
+ the family snow trip

In the next column indicate which traditions are your family's
favorites, why they are meaningful and enjoyable, what food makes the
occasion special, what values are taught and reinforced, and which ones

are important for your children to carry on. Consider whether your traditions are too burdensome to you, your family, or extended family. Evaluate carefully how to revise your traditions, if needed, to make them less burdensome and more meaningful.

Consider adding new traditions that are special to your family such as

- a "special plate" for special recognition
- father's blessing on the first day of school or when leaving home
- family service projects (not just at Christmas time)
- receiving a new set of scriptures at a particular milestone
- a special dress or a new suit for a child's eighth birthday
- special getaways for graduates or anniversaries
- Birthday traditions could be enhanced by re-telling the story of when your child was born, decorating the child's room in the middle of the night, writing a letter to your child each year, letting the birthday child choose a special meal, gathering with relatives, and, of course, a day off from chores.

In creating traditions, you need to make them fun and uniquely special to your family. They do not need to be extravagant. Remember, the best family traditions are those which reinforce your family's values, increase love, build self-esteem and security, and tie generations together. After you have chosen the family traditions you want to carry on or begin, write them on your calendar (year after year) so they will be planned and carried out.

Righteous Traditions

date ....

....
....
....
....
....
....
....
....
....
....
....
....
....
....
....
....
....
....
....
....
....
....
....
....

THIRTY-THREE

Practice Patience

*"We will have genuine joy and happiness
only as we learn patience."*

JOSEPH B. WIRTHLIN

GOAL: Learn to recognize when you are being impatient, and practice having patience this week.

I'm afraid that the phrase my children heard the most when they were young was "hurry up." They were never hurrying as fast as I thought they should be. Whether it was getting dressed, eating, or putting on shoes, all I remember saying was "hurry up," "hurry up," and "hurry up."

I finally realized that I wasn't letting my children enjoy their childhood. I was forcing them to adhere to my time schedule, and if they were dawdling while putting on their shoes, then maybe they needed that time to daydream, analyze, or just to think about things.

Recognize the times this week when you are impatient, and make an effort to practice patience. Patience is "a willingness, in a sense, to watch the unfolding purposes of God with a sense of wonder and awe."[1]

Children need time to motivate *themselves* to get going. They do not need to be continually nagged. They need to learn the way they like to put on their own clothes, the easiest way to put on their socks, the way they like to brush their teeth, or the way they like to eat their food. Understand that your children are continually learning, and even though it may appear they are dawdling, remember they are only children, and then *simply smile*.

Practicing patience is a difficult thing as we tend to revert to our old habits. Remember this is only for a week. As long as you are practicing patience with your children, try being patient with yourself as well. If *you* make a mistake, shrug it off, as you are still learning and have not yet reached perfection.

Be sure to note what kind of difference this makes in your children, your family, and yourself this week.

Notes:
1.   Neal A. Maxwell, "Patience," *Ensign*, Oct. 1980, 28.

Practice Patience

date ....

....
....
....
....
....
....
....
....
....
....
....
....
....
....
....
....
....
....
....
....
....
....
....
....
....
....

Sabbath Delight

"In this day of increasing access to and preoccupation with materialism, there is a sure protection for ourselves and our children against the plagues of our day. The key to that sure protection surprisingly can be found in Sabbath observance."

JAMES E. FAUST

GOAL: Plan your Sabbath day to be a "delight" that you and your family can enjoy and look forward to.

One day my son asked me why we couldn't be a "normal family" and play on Sundays. I tried to convince him that we are a "normal family" that chooses to obey God's commandments by keeping the Sabbath day holy. However, I feel his pain as he sees his neighborhood friends playing on Sundays and he longs to be with them. We can all sympathize with children and the "torture" they sometimes endure on the Sabbath.

This week, your challenge is to make the Sabbath a more enjoyable day for you and your family. Begin with an FHE lesson focusing on the Sabbath day.[1]

Start the day off right by playing uplifting music for your family to wake up to. This sets a good tone for the morning. Don't be surprised if your children moan and groan about the music (that's their job). Rest assured that when your children are older and leave home, their Sundays will not be complete without Sabbath music, and they will reminisce of their wonderful home.

Dedicate time to your family on the Sabbath:
- Ask your children and husband what they learned in church.
- Listen to their responses and ask thought-provoking questions.
- Review your children's progress in Scouting, Young Women Personal Progress, Duty to God, and Faith in God programs.
- Listen to your children play musical instruments.
- Play games together.
- Watch family videos and eat popcorn.
- Make cookies.

Make Sunday enjoyable for *you* by taking time to do things *you* want to do such as:

- family-focused scrap booking
- write in your journal
- research family history
- plan FHE
- review your Parenting Goals
- organize yourself for the week with meal plans, calendars, schedules, and activity planning

Proper Sabbath observance also includes spending time on your "knees in prayer, preparing lessons, studying the gospel, meditating, visiting the ill and distressed, writing letters to missionaries, taking a nap, reading wholesome material, and attending all the meetings of that day . . . ," and all this is to be done "with cheerful hearts and countenances (D&C 59:15)."[2]

A good end to the day is to have an enjoyable, relaxing meal with the family, "prepared with singleness of heart" (D&C 59:13). Prepare as much of the meal as possible the day before. Be sure to recruit everyone's help when it is time to clear the table and clean dishes afterwards.

Strive to make the Sabbath a "delight," and a day the Lord intended for it to be: "a day appointed unto you to rest from your labors, and to pay thy devotions unto the Most High" (D&C 59:10).

Notes:
1. *FHE Resource Book*, Lesson Ideas, "Sabbath," 218–219.
2. Spencer W Kimball, "The Sabbath—A Delight," *Ensign*, Jan. 1978, 1–5.

Sabbath Delight

date ....

....
....
....
....
....
....
....
....
....
....
....
....
....
....
....
....
....
....
....
....
....
....

Purposefully Ignore

"Also take no heed unto all words that are spoken"

ECCLESIASTES 7:21

GOAL: Choose one act of bad behavior that your children (or child) participate in, and focus on ignoring this behavior.

All children are inevitably going to have times of bad feelings toward situations and other people. However, they need to learn to work these feelings out on their own, and not pull you into their little tyrannical world.

I have heard over and over that if you want to stop your children's bad behavior, then you need to simply *ignore* the bad behavior. As I have learned, this is easier said than done. When your children are accustom to getting a predicted response from you by the way they act, and when you stop playing your part, they tend to exaggerate the bad behavior and wait for you to intervene—as you have always done.

This week analyze your children's behavior and decide on one bad behavior to ignore this week. It may be one child's particular behavior, or a behavior that your children collectively contribute to.

The danger here is that once you have decided to ignore your children's bad behavior, *you cannot give in.* If at any point you give in, your little actor or actress will determine that their behavior must get worse in order to have you intervene in the future. Remember that once you have chosen to ignore a behavior, the only time you are ever allowed to intervene is if there is imminent danger.

If your children whine, sulk, or throw temper tantrums, and you have chosen to ignore these behaviors, you must absolutely ignore them as if they were not behaving at all. Explain that you will not talk or pay attention while they are exhibiting these bad behaviors, and then say nothing more.

If at any time you start to feel aggravated by a particular child's bad behavior, put distance between yourself and the performer. If you are in public, don't walk too far away, but put distance between yourself and the child. At home, go into the bathroom, lock the door, and turn on the water or shower, and read a book if you have to. If the behavior continues, and *before* it makes you upset, send the child to his or her room, or somewhere to finish out their performance without bothering you.

When your children finish their performances, and all encores are over, follow up with a calm discussion about their behavior. Let your children know that if they choose to behave that way again, you will not pay any attention to them.

Purposefully Ignore

date ....

....
....
....
....
....
....
....
....
....
....
....
....
....
....
....
....
....
....
....
....
....
....
....
....

Blessed Bedtime

"Bedtime should be the best time. Those quiet moments at the close of noisy days can be rich opportunities to recall beauty, share disappointment, correct confusion, reaffirm affection, and tuck little ones cozily between blankets of security and peace."

KATHY CLAYTON (*as quoted by* CARY GRUBBLE)

GOAL: Make bedtime a pleasant end to the day by establishing a bedtime routine.

Bedtime can be either a very warm, loving time, or a crazy, upsetting part of your day. If you have had a particularly chaotic day, the bedtime hour can be your saving grace. After getting your little ones off to bed, you can relax, put your feet up, and enjoy some peace and quiet. Unfortunately, not all children are anxious to head off to bed and some will use every excuse to prolong their departure.

If your children choose bedtime as their last crusade of the day and consistently dawdle and try your patience, then this week you are going to make a plan to diffuse this battle.

First of all, prepare a bedtime schedule (as you did in chapter 4) by identifying the time children are expected to be securely in bed. Work backwards from this time, listing all the things that you and your children must accomplish prior to this time. If your children are old enough, you could post this schedule so they can follow it themselves. Try not to make bedtime seem like a punishment, but rather a loving, winding-down time of the day.

Within your prepared schedule, you may want to include activities such as:

+ bathing
+ getting in pajamas
+ setting out the next day's clothes
+ gathering backpacks, books and papers
+ picking up toys
+ getting a last cup of milk
+ brushing teeth
+ using the bathroom

- saying prayers
- reading a story
- singing a song
- reviewing their day's activities
- sharing their happiest moment of the day
- resolving any disputes of the day
- praising them for good deeds or accomplishments
- giving hugs and kisses
- telling them that you love them

To help children wind down and prepare for bed, do not let them watch television, rough-house, or contend with each other, or with you.

Keep in mind that teenagers are even more receptive and willing to communicate during a bedside chat. You may want to covertly work this into your time with them.

After the appointed bedtime has passed, if your children continue to play their games and demand interaction with you, it is fair and appropriate to "shut off" as a parent. If they call for you, do not answer. If they get up, send them back to bed without any emotion on your part. If they ask for a drink, remind them that according to the schedule, they should have already had one, and do not need another one.

Be strict about bedtime. You may even need to include "bedtime rules" in your Family Rule Book. A consistent bedtime is not only beneficial for the children, it gives you time to take a breath, regenerate, and spend time with your spouse.

Blessed Bedtime

date ....

....
....
....
....
....
....
....
....
....
....
....
....
....
....
....
....
....
....
....
....
....
....
....

THIRTY-SEVEN

Car Trouble

*"Each year an estimated 284,000 distracted drivers
are involved in serious highway crashes."*

AAA FOUNDATION FOR TRAFFIC SAFETY

GOAL: Make a plan to keep peace in the car.

Driver inattention is a major contributor to highway crashes. A highway safety study disclosed that the top two major distractions while driving are cell phones and gadgets, followed by children. This study also revealed that certain types of distractions are more prominent in certain age groups, for example, among 20- to 29-year-olds, *other occupants* such as young children often cause a distraction prior to an accident.[1]

There is nothing worse than being in a hot, cramped car with fighting children, while simultaneously negotiating heavy traffic.

You have a *responsibility* to drive and maneuver your car safely through traffic without your children being a distraction. Children need to understand that their parent's full attention must be on driving and not refereeing the fight or problem that is erupting in the backseat. They need to understand that their behavior could put themselves and others in serious danger.

If this is not a challenge in your family, consider yourself lucky. But if it is, you need to find the solution that works best for your family. Give one or more of the following methods a try this week:

- Make the children promise before they get in the car to be nice to one another, and go over rules and consequences for bad behavior.
- Pull the car over to the side of the road and give everyone a time-out for a pre-determined period of time.
- Return to the starting point of the trip, and try again to get to your destination without any contention (this probably would not work on long road trips).
- Have assigned seats, which change on a weekly or monthly basis
- Play classical music in the car.
- Listen to books on tape.
- If nothing else works, buy a bigger car so no child has to sit

directly next to another—they can keep their arms and legs in their own space, and breathe their own share of the air. I'm still waiting for the self-contained cubicles inside the car, with sound-proof dividers to keep the children from interacting with each other and the driver.

Whatever method you decide on, add this to your Family Rule Book, along with the agreed upon consequences if needed. (You might even get a free car wash out of this.)

Notes:

1. Study conducted by the University of North Carolina Highway Safety Research Center, in Chapel Hill, North Carolina, May 4, 2007, funded by the AAA Foundation for Traffic Safety.

Car Trouble

date..................................

....
....
....
....
....
....
....
....
....
....
....
....
....
....
....
....
....
....
....
....
....
....
....
....
....

Loads of Laughter

*"A wholesome sense of humor will be a safety valve
that will enable you to apply the lighter touch to heavy
problems and to learn some lessons in problem solving
that 'sweat and tears' often fail to dissolve."*

HUGH B. BROWN

GOAL: This week make a conscious effort to *laugh out loud* often. Laugh at yourself, laugh at situations, and encourage your children to laugh at whatever challenges come their way.

Teaching your children to have a sense of humor and laugh at themselves, to laugh at the right situations, and to not take anything too personally is a life-long survival skill. Laughter has been clinically found to increase our resistance to pain, reduce stress, improve our immune system, and make us feel better physically. This, together with easing tension, relieving awkward or embarrassing situations, and even changing attitudes, makes *learning to laugh invaluable*.

Kick off this light-hearted week with a FHE lesson emphasizing a sense of humor with suggestions found in the FHE Resource Book.[1]

Teach your children (and yourself) to find the humor in all situations. Teach them to laugh at their own mistakes—cleaning up a spilled beverage is a lot easier while laughing at it. It's painless to face your friends after tripping on your own shoelaces when you have rolled on the ground in laughter. Teach children that a properly developed sense of humor is sensitive to others' feelings while adding zest and enthusiasm to life.

The best way to teach is by example. When you drop something, make a mistake, say the wrong thing, or have a difficult encounter, just laugh at yourself. Laugh at the jokes your children tell you and share jokes in return. Initiate the "joke of the day" that you post, recap, and laugh at throughout the day.

Make it clear there is also a time not to laugh. Teach your children to never make family or friends the object of a joke, nor should they embarrass someone in front of others—*even teasing can be hurtful*. As the FHE lesson points out, we should not participate in humor that degrades, is based on indecent situations, makes fun of another's physical limitations, handicaps, ethnic, racial, religious differences, or of anything sacred.[2]

> *Be sensitive to teenagers who might believe you are laughing "at their expense." If teenagers can develop a healthy sense of humor, perhaps they will not take themselves too seriously, and the teenage years will not be so brutal.*

Notes:
1.   *FHE Resource Book*, Lesson Ideas, "Sense of Humor," 197–198.
2.   Ibid.

Loads of Laughter

date ....

....

....

....

....

....

....

....

....

....

....

....

....

....

....

....

....

....

....

....

....

....

....

....

Don't Stress It

"Ask yourself, 'Who will even know or care in a
hundred years?' That's one way to separate the things
that really matter from those that don't."

ERIC STEPHAN

GOAL: Adopt a more relaxed attitude toward life this week.

Warning: If you are a type "A" personality, this week might possibly kill you. With a little luck you will learn a few valuable lessons and come away a better person and mother.

Do you find yourself so stressed and frazzled that you barely have time to breathe? Moms who are uptight unknowingly pass this stress on to their children; they set expectations too high and tend to miss out on a lot of genuine fun and enjoyment. The more you learn to prepare in advance and take life in stride, the better example you will set and the more easy-going and even-tempered your children will be.

Purposefully make this a s-l-o-w week. Don't schedule anything. If you have appointments planned, consider rescheduling for another week. For the out-of-home commitments you do have, leave early, giving yourself time to safely drive and more casually walk. Don't try to fit in too many errands into a short period of time.

Make sure you have on-hand the ingredients needed to make simple, family-favorite meals. Try to prepare the family meals early in the day to avoid the before-dinner rush. Take the time to sit down and eat each meal unhurried with your family.

Make plans to:
+ go to bed early
+ get enough sleep
+ set your alarm a little earlier than usual to give yourself extra time to get going
+ iron your clothes the night before they are needed, or wear something that doesn't need ironing
+ start early on tasks or projects with deadlines such as Sunday lessons, talks, and planning activities
+ deliberately sit still and think.

Breathing is also an important part of developing a relaxed outlook. Whenever you think about it, deliberately breathe, relax your shoulders, and push them down a little, roll your head, and stretch your neck, let your arms and fingers hang down, and notice the blood rushing to your fingertips. Take a deeper breath and exhale completely. Then remember to *simply smile!*

To help experience less stress this week:

+ Make sure you walk at a more relaxed pace.
+ Walk to the mailbox slowly.
+ Take a slow walk with your children.
+ Do your shopping slowly.

When things go wrong—and they will—don't react or fly off the handle. *Simply smile*, and then calmly decide how best to handle the problem.

Help your children see the benefits of preparing early to avoid last-minute stress.

+ Set their alarms earlier, so they get up early and are not rushing to get out the door.
+ Walk them slowly to school or the bus stop.
+ Encourage them to start early on homework and projects to avoid being frantic on the due date, causing you stress as well.

In considering the results of this week ask yourself: Did you notice less stress in home? How did your children respond? How was your attitude? Did anything important get missed? Could you continue this way of life? Would you want to continue this way of life?

Don't Stress It

date ....

....

....

....

....

....

....

....

....

....

....

....

....

....

....

....

....

....

....

....

....

....

....

....

....

Telephone Etiquette

"I was called many times and I would not hear"

ALMA 10:6

GOAL: Teach your children proper telephone etiquette and put an end to inappropriate interruptions while you are using the phone.

Just as Pavlov's dog reacted to a ringing bell by salivating, so it seems that children respond to a ringing phone by demanding their parent's immediate attention. For some reason, that is the time they *urgently* need something from Mom or Dad. In a family meeting, discuss with your children how they should act when you—or anyone for that matter—are using the telephone. Emphasize that they should use their indoor voices so the person using the telephone can hear the person on the other end. If your children absolutely must talk to you, encourage them to quietly raise their hand. Acknowledge them with a nod of your head to indicate that you will talk to them as soon as you are off the phone. If they continue to interrupt you, the consequence listed in the rule book will result. After you have had a successful telephone call, remember to *praise* your children for respecting the telephone rules.

If your children are old enough, teach them the correct method to answer the phone, what information to give, and what not to give. Stress the importance of writing all messages down and verifying the correct name and telephone number of the caller. Make sure they know how to appropriately make a phone call and especially emergency phone calls. Keep a list of numbers by the telephone including emergency numbers, friends, neighbors, and how they can get a hold of you and your husband at all times. Make sure your children ask permission before using the phone, until they are old enough to use proper judgment.

Also, evaluate how much *your* life is ruled by the telephone. You may want to make a rule that the telephone does not get answered during the dinner hour or after a certain time at night. Make a point to never answer the phone as you are running out the door or when spending special time with your children.

For a fun activity, let your children take turns recording the message on the family answering machine.

Telephone Etiquette

date......................................

....
....
....
....
....
....
....
....
....
....
....
....
....
....
....
....
....
....
....
....
....
....
....
....

Individual Interviews

*"Personal interviews are an important resource in
maintaining the integrity of our fortress. Through
them, we . . . learn about [our children's] problems and
concerns, establish open communication and trust that
will enable us to foresee any danger, help them make
decisions, and support them during difficult times."*

HORACIO A. TENORIO

GOAL: Hold a personal interview with each of your children to assess how they are doing in all areas of their life.

Holding personal interviews with your children will give them a sense of accountability and help them learn to make goals and follow through. Some families hold regular interviews the first Sunday of the month, while others report success with a weekly meeting.

This meeting can be as formal or informal as you would like, depending on each child. Some children benefit from a formal meeting that begins and ends with a prayer, and where topics, ideas, and goals are written down. Other children benefit from an informal meeting, perhaps just sitting on the front porch and having a talk. However, it is good for the parent to later write down the ideas and goals that were discussed so they don't forget and can ask about them later. More often than not, children benefit from having a one-on-one interview with only one parent. This way your children don't feel out-numbered or feel a need to be defensive.

Start the interview off with a *smile* and *positive comment* which praises them for something they have done. Then discuss topics such as:

+ friends
+ school
+ church
+ scouting
+ youth programs
+ sports
+ pets
+ chores
+ music lessons and progress

- plans for the future
- interests and ambitions
- areas they need to work on

Help them set short- and long-term goals. Make sure you address any problems you have noticed and give ideas on how to improve. Try to be observant during the week(s) prior to the interview so you can discuss with your child anything you notice and feel needs to be discussed.

Instead of overwhelming your child with a lot of topics, you could choose to focus on only a few, such as school, scouting, and one particular area that your child is struggling with.

If you discover that your children greatly benefit from this meeting, consider scheduling future meetings on your calendar so these interviews will not be forgotten or overlooked.

Individual Interviews

date ....

....
....
....
....
....
....
....
....
....
....
....
....
....
....
....
....
....
....
....
....
....
....
....
....

FORTY TWO

Be Grateful

*"Thinking of things we are grateful for is a healing balm. It helps
us get outside ourselves. It changes our focus from our pains and
our trials to the abundance of this beautiful world we live in."*

JOSEPH B. WIRTHLIN

GOAL: Sow seeds of gratitude in your children.

People who focus on what they have, rather than what they don't have, are much happier and more content than those who continually want more. By teaching your children gratitude, you are teaching a life-skill that will benefit them for the rest of their lives. People naturally want to be around others who are happy and grateful.

Start the week off with a family lesson on gratitude. To enhance your FHE lesson include one or more of the following activities:

+ Make a list of blessings—this can be done individually or collectively as a family.
+ Have your family make a collage of things they are thankful for.
+ Make a gratitude box where family members write (or draw) something they are grateful for on a piece of paper and put it in the box. At the next family meeting, the box is opened and all of the slips of paper are read out loud. (This would be a great activity for the month of November, with the slips of paper read on Thanksgiving Day).
+ Help your children write a thank-you note to someone that has helped them in some way.
+ Help your children make a treat for homebound neighbors or nursing home residents.
+ Help your family sort through their closets for clothes to be donated to a local charity.

At the end of each day, ask your children what they were thankful for that day. Share with them what you were thankful for. Encourage your children to express their gratitude in their prayers as well.

As you go throughout the week, let your children hear you express your thanks and gratitude through actions, word, and prayer.

Be Grateful

date ....

....
....
....
....
....
....
....
....
....
....
....
....
....
....
....
....
....
....
....
....
....
....
....
....

FORTY-THREE

Quiet Time

*"Spending a few moments in a peaceful
setting is a relaxing experience."*

ERIC STEPHAN

GOAL: Schedule a period each day that is reserved for quiet time.

Children do not get enough time to think, daydream, or ponder. They demand to be constantly entertained, and today's society caters to this demand. Having quiet time teaches children to be comfortable with silence and gives them time to think and be receptive to the spirit. Most importantly, mothers need quiet time for their own mental wellness and rejuvenation.

Just as you developed a schedule in chapter 4, create another one that sets aside specific time for quiet time—time especially for *you*. Instruct your children that during this time they need to keep themselves busy by napping, reading a book, drawing, coloring, playing quietly, or participating in some other appropriate activity for their age and interest.

Quiet time usually works best right after lunch (when children are less likely to be asking for food or drink) and could last anywhere from thirty minutes to a couple hours, depending on the ages and capabilities of your children. You may need to start with just a small amount of time and work up to a longer period. Make sure your children understand that this is "quiet time" and that you do not want to be interrupted during this time.

It is a good idea to set and use a timer so the children understand there is a time limit and know when it is alright to interrupt you again. You could also elect to not answer the phone or doorbell during this time.

You may determine that the period before bedtime is better for quiet time. This provides wind-down time, and if smaller children have gone or are going to bed it keeps the older ones quiet.

Make quiet time *your* special time of the day, to do only what *you* want to do.

Quiet Time

date ....

....
....
....
....
....
....
....
....
....
....
....
....
....
....
....
....
....
....
....
....
....
....
....
....
....

FORTY-FOUR

Ask Questions

*"[Asking] questions . . . help[s] them feel like they
share in the control and, at the same time, help
them learn to make responsible decisions."*

C. RICHARD CHIDESTER

GOAL: Instead of your children always asking you questions, ask your children the questions, and get them thinking.

At a certain point in parenthood, we all experience children who seems to ask "Why?" all day long. Children are curious creatures who are eager to learn all they can. They love to explore the world around them, just as much as they love to have attention from their parents. Both of these factors result in the "why factor." No parent wants to curtail their child's curiosity, but a non-stop barrage of being asked "why" can be exhausting if not down-right ridiculous.

To foster your child's curiosity and reasoning ability—instead of you answering the infamous "Why?" or other questions—turn to your children with questions of your own:

+ What can you do about that?
+ What do you think would happen if you did that?
+ What else can you try?
+ Why do you think it works that way?
+ What do you think would be best in this situation?
+ Is there a better way to do that?
+ How do you think that will make others feel?
+ How can you learn more about that?
+ When would be a better time to do that?

When you ask your children questions, it trains them to think on their own and evaluate alternatives when solving their own problems. What do you think?

Ask Questions

date ....

....
....
....
....
....
....
....
....
....
....
....
....
....
....
....
....
....
....
....
....
....
....
....
....
....
....

FORTY-FIVE

Serve One Another

*"But ye will teach them to walk in the ways of truth
and soberness . . . and to serve one another."*

MOSIAH 4:15

GOAL: Provide opportunities for your children to learn about the joys of serving each other.

Service among family members helps create a charitable, harmonious, and loving environment. Large acts of service bring the family closer together as a whole, but it's the smaller, more personal acts of service that teach your children how to be less self-centered and think of others.

This week will require some planning on your part as you create opportunities for family members to serve each other. You may want to start the week off with a FHE lesson on service.[1] During FHE, introduce one of the service ideas listed below.

- **Create "pass-it-on cards."** Whenever you do a secret service for someone, leave one of these cards that challenges the recipient to perform a secret act of service for another person within the next twenty-four hours, and pass the card along to the next recipient of secret service.
- **Make a "recognition jar."** Whenever someone sees another doing a good deed, write it on a piece of paper and add it to the jar, which is then opened and read at the next family meeting.
- **Have "secret siblings."** Each sibling (parents may participate also) draws the name of another. During the week they are to provide secret service for that sibling. At the next FHE they should guess who their secret sibling was. Make sure you remind, encourage, and follow-up with each child during the week to make sure everyone is providing secret service.

In addition to the above, encourage your children to help each other as the week goes along. When one child is too small to get a snack or drink for themselves, have an older child help them out. Persuade your older siblings to help the younger siblings with homework or chores. Make sure you recognize their efforts by praise and in the recognition jar.

If you or your children are having a hard day, go out of your way to

113

give service to someone else. By serving someone else you look beyond your own troubles and your own burdens become easier to bear.

In addition to your children serving each other, plan a few secret service acts you could perform for your extended family, friends, or neighbors.

Notes:
1. *FHE Resource Book*, Lesson 17, "Love at Home," 74.

Serve One Another

date ....

....
....
....
....
....
....
....
....
....
....
....
....
....
....
....
....
....
....
....
....
....
....
....
....
....

FORTY SIX

Go One-on-One

"Without this one-on-one counseling together with our
children, they are prone to believe that Dad and Mom . . .
don't understand or care about the challenges they are facing."

ROBERT D. HALES

GOAL: Schedule and enjoy one-on-one time with each child.

Your child's self-esteem is greatly boosted when you spend one-on-one time with him. This one-on-one time is different from the reconnecting you did in chapter 23, as this is a planned activity that you participate in for a longer period of time.

With your calendar in hand, schedule a time this week that you can devote to each child. Make it a special outing for the child such as:

+ going out to lunch
+ going for an ice cream cone
+ taking in a movie
+ playing at the park
+ exploring the zoo
+ building sand castles at the beach
+ simply ask your child what they would like to do

When you schedule time with your child—and stick to it; it shows that you care enough to slip away from the hectic stresses of daily life to do something just with them.

If "going out" doesn't work, then plan special time at home. For example:

+ throw the football
+ shoot hoops
+ work on a favorite hobby
+ build something together
+ bike around the neighborhood
+ go for a walk in the rain and splash in the puddles
+ bake a batch of cookies
+ jump in piles of leaves
+ dive into a hot-fudge sundae together
+ split a piece of pie

+ spend time sitting beside his bed before he goes to sleep and share the events of his day

Use this one-on-one time to get to know each child. Find out your child's favorite color, television show, game, book, sport, ice cream flavor(s), and share your favorites as well. Inquire about your child's friends, school, church activities, and other interests. Be excited about their life and spend time listening to and talking about them.

> *Do not plan activities that could breed disagreement for your one-on-one time (such as food or clothes shopping), as it is easy for disagreement, frustration, and resentment to creep in and thwart your efforts.*

Go One-on-One

date ....

....

....

....

....

....

....

....

....

....

....

....

....

....

....

....

....

....

....

....

....

Emergency Essentials

"If ye are prepared ye shall not fear."

D & C 38:30

GOAL: Teach your children and review with them the basic procedures of responding to an emergency.

Very young children have been credited with saving a life by knowing what to do in an emergency. Children are never too young to learn, and children feel more secure if they know what to do in the event of an emergency.

Arrange a family meeting and, at the very least, discuss these fundamental topics:

1. The emergency response telephone numbers for your area (usually 911), when to call, and especially when not to call.
2. Emergency escape routes for each room of the home. Each room needs two exits. If one of the exits is from a high window, make sure there is an escape ladder available.
3. Designated meeting place once the family evacuates the home.
4. What neighbors the children can turn to if you are not home during an emergency.
5. How to deal with a small fire on the stove or in the oven.
6. How to deal with emergencies common to the area in which you live—such as earthquakes, tornadoes, hurricanes, flooding, or wildfires—whether you are at home or away.
7. What to expect and do if an emergency occurs while your children are at school. Decide how you will reunite.
8. If your children are old enough, show them where the circuit breaker or fuse box is and how to use it. Explain how and when to shut off the water and how to use a fire extinguisher.
9. The telephone number(s) where your children can reach you. If your phone has a memory system, program your contact numbers so that your youngest child will have to remember only 1 digit. (Remember that programmed or cordless phones may not work during a power outage).

Conduct a few emergency drills at home, so when an emergency really

119

occurs, your children will be less frightened and will be capable of calmly acting according to the plan they are familiar with.

> The FHE Resource Book includes family preparedness activities and information on pages 322–340.

Emergency Essentials

date ....

....
....
....
....
....
....
....
....
....
....
....
....
....
....
....
....
....
....
....
....
....
....
....

FORTY-EIGHT

Pick Your Battles

"Ye shall not need to fight in this battle:
set yourselves, stand ye still …"

2 CHRONICLES 20:17

GOAL: Objectively observe situations and determine if it is right to intervene or take action.

We all know that children, just like adults, are going to have bad days. Some days Mom is just too tired to deal with the problem at hand. Ultimately, not every battle is worth fighting.

This week you are to stop, watch, and analyze the conflicts that may erupt. As you watch, take a moment before you react, and ask yourself:

+ Is this a problem I need to stop now, or can my children deal with this on their own?
+ Have my children been taught enough skills to handle this situation?
+ Are they capable of better behavior? (Remember to take into consideration the age of your children and their developmental level.)
+ Are they trying to get my attention?
+ Is this the way I want them to get my attention?
+ Are they tired?
+ Are they hungry?
+ Are they bored?
+ Do they need fresh air?
+ Do they need some time by themselves?

After your objective analysis, you may determine that the problem at hand warrants attention. Legitimate problems need to be dealt with in their early stages. Good authority has shown that if you don't stop a problem immediately, it will be ten times harder to stop the next time. Consider whether you really want to deal with this problem an additional ten times.

Sometimes taking a step back and analyzing the entire situation gives you a better perspective and a better approach on how to deal with the battle that is raging.

Pick Your Battles

date ....

....
....
....
....
....
....
....
....
....
....
....
....
....
....
....
....
....
....
....
....
....
....
....
....
....

Mind Your Manners

*"Courtesy is a natural outgrowth of the refining
influence of the Spirit of the Lord."*

BRUCE R. MCCONKIE

GOAL: Teach (or reteach) your children the basic manners of society.

As soon as children start talking, they should learn to say "please" and "thank you." If you start young, good manners will become automatic. Teaching good manners to your children will help boost their confidence; they will know how to approach and interact with others and will make your home life much more pleasant.

A great start this week would be a family lesson on manners and courtesy. In addition to the *Family Home Evening Resource Manual* there are fantastic books at the library on manners, courtesy, and etiquette.[1] A fun way for the family to learn courtesy is through role playing, which can be incorporated into your FHE lesson, or during a family "manners meal."

Basic Courtesy Rules:
+ Smile and make eye-contact upon meeting someone.
+ Hold the door and offer chairs to others, especially Mother, Father, and elderly people.
+ Say "please" and "thank you," "excuse me," and "I'm sorry" when appropriate.
+ Keep bodily function noises quiet.
+ Do not interrupt. (This topic was addressed previously chapter 17.)
+ Write a thank-you note when a gift is received.

During the week, encourage your children (and yourself) to follow the courtesy rules. If your children forget, kindly remind them of the correct behavior, and make sure they follow through.

Above all, be a good example of what you teach.

Notes:
1. *FHE Resource Book*, Lesson Ideas, "Manners," 204–205.

Mind Your Manners

date ....

....
....
....
....
....
....
....
....
....
....
....
....
....
....
....
....
....
....
....
....
....
....
....
....

FIFTY

Express Yourself

*"But did pour out their hearts to him; and he
did know the thoughts of their hearts."*

MOSIAH 24:12

GOAL: Before frustration and overwhelming emotions set in with your children, sit down, and encourage them to *talk* to you about their *feelings*.

Young children can have very strong feelings and emotions that they don't yet know how to deal with. As a result, children feel powerless and have a propensity to act out these feelings in uncontrolled or unsuitable ways.

Focus this week on encouraging your children to sit down with you and express their feelings. Look for times when they are beginning to show signs of frustration or being troubled. Immediately take them aside—into another room if needed—and encourage them to sit down with you and peacefully discuss how they are feeling. If they are too young or too upset to fully vocalize what they are feeling, kindly and calmly talk them through their feelings. Asking them yes or no questions to which they only need to respond with a nod or shake of their head helps them calm down and learn to deal with their feelings.

When you feel yourself becoming frustrated or upset, you also need to try to talk about your feelings. If you are upset at a particular child (or spouse), sit down with that child (or spouse) and tell him or her how you are feeling. Try to start your statements with "I" followed by a feeling word. For example: "I feel sad when you say such mean things to your sister." This method avoids finger-pointing and keeps the other person from feeling defensive. You are simply letting them know how you are *feeling*.

If you have a child who continues to misbehave, try the "I" method to express your feelings and see if you can reach a better conclusion than before. Another example: "I am upset when you don't do your chores as we agreed. What can we do to get your chores done?"

This is an important concept and teaching our children how to manage their emotions through expressing their feelings appropriately is an important step in developing self-control, and ultimately building self-esteem.

Express Yourself

....
....
....
....
....
....
....
....
....
....
....
....
....
....
....
....
....
....
....
....
....
....
....
....

Discover Nature

*"Cultivating wonder about nature heightens our appreciation
of all creation and begins to break down our artificial
distinctions between things temporal and spiritual."*

SHARON DEQUER

GOAL: Take your children outside every day to discover nature.

Fresh air and sunlight add to an overall stimulus that will increase a children's immune system, regulate their biological clock, improve their attention span and self-control, boost their academic performance, and teach them to play more creatively and handle stress more effectively. Despite these wonderful benefits, an alarming amount of children spend their free time indoors, thereby depriving themselves of numerous physical and mental health benefits.

You may already take your children to the park or other places, but make plans this week to take your children outside and get them excited about nature.

A good way to start this week is by teaching an FHE lesson about nature.[1]

Plan an outdoor activity for each day that will have a dedicated period of time. It would be fun to also plan some activities for the nighttime.

Some activities may include:
+ a trip to the park
+ having a picnic
+ riding bikes
+ hiking
+ watching the clouds
+ bird watching
+ camping
+ enjoying a sunset
+ gazing at the stars and enjoying the moon
+ boating
+ fishing
+ working together in the garden
+ planting a tree

- climbing a tree
- rolling down a grassy hill
- playing backyard games

Don't rush these outings. Take time to:
- look at the leaves
- watch an ant on the sidewalk
- hold a roly-poly bug
- watch a ladybug
- watch the clouds
- listen to the birds
- smell the flowers
- roll in the grass
- examine rocks
- wiggle your feet in the sand

Depending on the season you could:
- dance in the rain
- rake leaves and jump in the piles
- make snow angels
- star gaze and look at the majestic snow-capped mountains

As you embark on your adventures, you may want to gather items to make a display on paper, in a glass vase, in a shadow box, or laminate as place mats to make your memories last.

Take the time to watch and enjoy the wonderment in your children's face as they discover God's creations.

Notes:
1. *FHE Resource Book,* Lesson 6, "Nature—Evidence of Heavenly Father's Love," 23.

Discover Nature

date ....

....
....
....
....
....
....
....
....
....
....
....
....
....
....
....
....
....
....
....
....
....
....
....
....

Say It Nicer

*"Teach your children never to speak unkindly to
others regarding members of the family."*

EZRA TAFT BENSON

GOAL: Teach your children to "say it nicer" when they speak rudely or make inappropriate demands.

Children can easily get in the habit of calling each other names or making rude comments when they are upset. Often these remarks range from the absurd to the down-right nasty. If not rectified at home, these offensive words and habits spill over into school, church, playtime, sports, and other areas. This behavior should be considered unacceptable at any time or place.

To combat this problem, encourage your children to "say it nicer" before they can continue with what they are doing. If your children say something mean or rude, require them to repeat what they have said, using kind words. Insist that your children repeat their words until they can "say it nicer," and it is acceptable. This is a good rule to be added to your Family Rule Book.

Be aware of the words you are using toward your children and husband this week also. Try to use the kind words you want your children to exhibit. Bind yourself to the "say it nicer" law as well.

Say It Nicer

date ....

....
....
....
....
....
....
....
....
....
....
....
....
....
....
....
....
....
....
....
....
....
....
....

Quotation Index

25. Anne C. Pingree, "Choose Ye Therefore Christ the Lord," *Ensign*, Nov. 2003, 110.

26. Boyd K. Packer, "Teach Them Correct Principles," *Ensign*, May 1990, 89.

27. James E. Faust, "The Greatest Challenge in the World—Good Parenting," *Ensign*, Nov. 1990, 32.

28. "Compassion: Feeling and Acting," *Ensign*, Apr. 1993, 67.

29. Gordon B. Hinckley, "Mormon Should Mean 'More Good,' " *Ensign*, Nov. 1990, 51.

30. L. Lionel Kendrick, "Christlike Communications," *Ensign*, Nov. 1988, 23.

31. Robert D. Hales, "With all the Feeling of a Tender Parent: A Message of Hope to Families," *Ensign*, May 2004, 88.

32. L. Tom Perry, "Family Traditions," *Ensign*, May 1990, 19.

33. Joseph B. Wirthlin, "Patience, a Key to Happiness," *Ensign*, May 1987, 30.

34. James E. Faust, "The Lord's Day," *Ensign*, Nov. 1991, 33.

35. Ecclesiastes 7:21

36. Cary Grubble (quoting Kathy Clayton) "To Be a Better Homemaker," *Ensign*, Jan. 1984, 67.

37. *AAA Foundation For Traffic Safety*, 2001; Study conducted by the University of North Carolina Highway Safety Research Center, in Chapel Hill, North Carolina, May 4, 2007, funded by the AAA Foundation for Traffic Safety.

38. Hugh B. Brown, in Conference Report, Apr. 1968, 100.

39. Eric Stephan, "Reducing Stress: Welcome Thoughts for the Over-Involved," *Ensign*, Apr. 1982, 22.

40. Alma 10:6

41. Horacio A. Tenorio, "Let Us Build Fortresses," *Ensign*, Nov. 1994, 23.

42. Joseph B. Wirthlin, "Improving Our Prayers," *Ensign*, Mar. 2004, 24.

43. *Ensign*, Apr. 1982, 22.

44. C. Richard Chidester, "The Fine Art of Raising Teenagers," *Ensign*, July 1981, 39.

45. Mosiah 4:15

46. Robert D. Hales, "With all the Feeling of a Tender Parent: A Message of Hope to Families," *Ensign*, May 2004, 88.

47. D&C 38:30

48. 2 Chronicles 20:17

49. Bruce R. McConkie, *Family Home Evening Resource Book*, 204

50. Alma 24:12

51. Sharon Dequer, "Discovering Nature," *Ensign*, June 1977, 54.

52. Ezra Taft Benson, "The Honored Place of Woman", *Ensign*, Nov. 1981, 104.

Janene Ustach

Photo by Susan St. John

Janene Ustach was raised in St. George, Utah, and graduated from Dixie College with an associate of science degree. She moved to California to continue her schooling at the University of West Los Angeles, and graduated with a bachelor's degree in paralegal studies.

While attending school in California, she met and later married her husband, Steve. They have four children: Nicholas, Matthew, Trenton, and Katelyn.

Janene enjoys a variety of sports, including basketball, swimming, racquetball, volleyball, and skiing. In her spare time she dabbles in gardening, home decorating, crafts, reading, and trying new recipes—much to the chagrin of her kids.

She has had numerous callings in her ward, and is currently serving as a Sunday School teacher and activity days leader.

Janene's first book, *My Self-Improvement Journal*, focuses on bettering oneself on a personal level. She has a strong testimony of self-improvement and goal setting that was instilled in her as a youth. It is her desire for all women to be the best that they can—and want—to be.